BIRTH ORDER AND YOU

Dr. Ronald W. Richardson
Lois A. Richardson, MA

DISCARD

Self-Counsel Press
(a division of)
International Self-Counsel Press Ltd.
Canada   USA

Self-Counsel Press acknowledges the financial support of the Government of Canada through the Book Publishing Industry Development Program (BPIDP) for our publishing activities.

Printed in Canada.

First edition: 1990
Reprinted: 1990; 1995; 1997
Second edition: 2000; 2004

Some of the material in this book first appeared, in slightly different form, in the chapter "Who's on First: Birth Order and Gender Position in the Family of Origin," by Lois Richardson in the book Family Ties That Bind, *by Dr. Ronald W. Richardson, published by Self-Counsel Press.*

Canadian Cataloguing in Publication Data

Richardson, Ronald W. (Ronald Wayne), 1939-
Birth order and you

(Self-counsel series)
Includes bibliographical references.
ISBN 1-55180-245-7

    1. Birth order — Psychological aspects.
I. Richardson, L.A. (Lois Ann), 1944-   II. Title.   III. Series.
BF723.B5R53 2000   155.9'24   C00-910549-2

The lengthy quote on page 238 is reprinted with permission from I Can't Stay Long *by Laurie Lee (Andre Deutsch Ltd., 1975.)*

Cartoons by Dave Alavoine

Self-Counsel Press
(a division of)
International Self-Counsel Press Ltd.

1704 N. State Street	1481 Charlotte Road
Bellingham, WA 98225	North Vancouver, BC V7J 1H1
USA	Canada

Contents

6   OLDEST BROTHERS

1
WHY BIRTH ORDER MATTERS

Give me a child for the first seven years and you may do what you like with him afterwards.

Jesuit saying

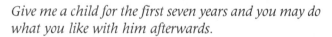

Aaron is 55 years old. He is a senior partner in a large, successful law firm in Pittsburgh, where he has worked since graduating from law school. He and his wife, Beatrice, his high school sweetheart, have two children now in university. Aaron is on the board of several non-profit agencies in Pittsburgh and is an elder in his church. He works most weekday evenings, but usually manages to play golf with important clients on Saturday. He gets up early every morning to swim.

Aaron and Beatrice have a cordial, but rather distant, relationship. Aaron is definitely the master of the house and was the disciplinarian when the children were young, punishing them more often and more severely than Beatrice would have wished. He loves his wife and children, but isn't able to express it very often in ways they can understand. He has high standards for them all and doesn't hesitate to let them know when they have failed to meet those standards. When Beatrice doesn't seem to have the household organized sufficiently well, Aaron feels let down. If the children get less than an A- in any course, he thinks they must be goofing off because he knows they are capable of doing much better.

He also drives himself hard at the office and expects his staff to do the same "for the sake of the firm." When his secretary of 10 years resigned recently, he felt personally betrayed and refused to attend her going-away luncheon. He prides himself on his own loyalty and has kept in touch with previous partners who retired after he started with the firm.

He dutifully visits his mother in a nursing home every week and pays her expenses. He had invited her to move into his home, but she didn't want to bother his family.

Brad is 53 years old, unmarried, and works as a shoe salesman. He owns a $30,000 sports car, but not his own home. He has more debts than he can handle, partly because of the amount he spends on cigarettes and drink. He is a chain-smoker and an unacknowledged alcoholic. He spends most evenings at the neighborhood pub. He gets along with almost anybody, and people genuinely like him when he's sober, but he often turns mean when he's been drinking. He has only a few friends who still tolerate him consistently.

He was involved for several years with a married woman at one of the shoe stores where he worked. When her husband found out about it, he was forced to quit his job there. He was on employment insurance for six months before he found another selling job.

Evelyn is 49 years old and looks 35. She is a vivacious, pretty, almost-natural blonde. She lives in Denver with her husband Lee. She moved away from her hometown when she was 18 to get away from her strict, domineering parents and has been back to visit only two or three times since.

When she works, Evelyn works as a receptionist; she prefers to stay home so she can ski in the winter and go to the beach in the summer.

She has been married and divorced twice and has recently married again. Her first two husbands just couldn't keep her happy and seemed too much like parents to her. She enjoyed the comfortable life she had with them, though, and didn't like having to work when she was between marriages.

As a young wife, she kept house half-heartedly and spent most of her free time visiting friends and going to parties. Her son by her first marriage spent half of his time with his father, though he worshipped his mother and as an adult enjoyed being her escort before she remarried. Although she often left him with babysitters when he was a child, Evelyn enjoys her son very much as an adult and has never been critical of anything he has done.

What do Aaron, Brad, and Evelyn have in common? Very little it seems. And yet they have the same parents and grew up in the same family just a few years apart. They are siblings — two brothers and a sister (in that order).

Your birth order position (whether born first, second, last, etc.), your sex (male or female), and the sex of your siblings affect the kind of person you become. The kind of people Aaron, Brad, and Evelyn have become is consistent with their birth order positions. They needed that particular mix of siblings to develop the personal characteristics they did. They would not have become the same people if they had not had each other.

People often say they can't understand "how people from the same family can be so different." What they don't realize is that each sibling is born into a different family. Each new child needs to create a unique identity, separate from the others. But this new identity is created within a context of those who are already there.

a. THE FAMILY CONTEXT

The people in a family change in many ways between the birth of each child. Their circumstances are different, their emotional life is different, and the world around them is different. These differences mean that each child is treated in a different way by parents and siblings, usually unintentionally.

In addition to the changes in the family itself between births, each child is born with a unique genetic inheritance and constitutional makeup. This also affects how family members relate to the child, which in turn affects the child's perception of all that happens in the family.

1.   Circumstantial differences

Where the family lives, what other relatives and friends are around, how much money is available, and the career stage of the parents are all factors that may change over time and will affect the early experiences of each child.

The family is, of course, numerically different for each sibling. A child who is born into a household with only two adults in it has a different experience of early childhood than the child born into a household of two adults and three children. Much of the influence of birth order on personality is due to this difference in who is physically present in the household.

A later child may also arrive when an elderly grandparent is either living with the family or placing many demands on the time and money of the parents as well as adding emotional strain to the family.

2.   Emotional differences

One of the greatest determinants of a child's personality development is the happiness level of the parents. The personal and marital fulfillment and contentment of the parents may be at a different level at each child's birth, and this will affect how they are as parents as well as the emotional atmosphere in the home.

A newly wed couple may be more loving to each other than a disillusioned couple suffering from the seven-year itch. A younger couple may still be working out their differences and power struggles and adjusting to each other, while an older couple may have made their peace with each other. A struggling student couple or a couple concerned about getting a career started will be different kinds of parents at that stage than they are when more established and comfortable.

The parents of later-born children have usually settled into their social roles and are more secure in their career directions. For each succeeding birth, the current family members bring a higher level of maturity to the experience of being a parent or being an older sibling.

The parents may develop somewhat different parenting styles between children. The first child is usually born to a youngish couple, with no experience in childrearing. The two of them now have to make space in their lives for a third (very demanding) person. It is normal for these parents to be anxious and uncertain with a tendency to focus much more attention on this child than they do on later children.

When the second child is born, the parents have some experience behind them. They are usually more relaxed about parenting and also less impressed with the child's stages of development (first words, first steps, first whatever). So the child who comes later tends to get less pressure but also less attention and affirmation for similar accomplishments.

When there are many years between the births of siblings, even things like a change in the prevailing theories of childrearing can make a difference in the way the siblings are raised.

3. The external world

Each child born into a family also faces a different external world. A child born in London during World War II had a different kind of early family experience than a younger sibling born in Canada after the war. A child who became a teenager in the political turmoil of the early seventies had a different experience from that of an older sibling who became a teenager in the Camelot years of the early sixties. A child born in the inflationary years of the eighties will have a different family context than a child born in the nineties.

b. FAMILY IDENTITY

The over-riding influence on an individual's development is the family personality. Children develop their social behavior by relating to their own parents and siblings. For instance, even though all oldest children are likely to share many characteristics, they are all also unique in the way those characteristics are expressed.

Even where non-birth order characteristics are the dominant element in someone's personality, some of the birth order traits are usually evident. For example, an exceptionally bright or talented youngest boy might still be more dependent or less responsible than the other children in his family. He may be a genius, but a spoiled, babied genius.

In addition, birth order doesn't determine the basic values of a person or the person's value to society. It affects social interactions more than attitudes and ethical stances. Depending on a number of other family and environmental circumstances, an only child can turn out to be Joseph Stalin or Leonardo da Vinci, Elvis Presley or Franklin Roosevelt. But these four men shared certain characteristics that are common to male only children.

c. SIBLING DISTINCTIVENESS

We each need to develop a distinctive identity or a separate sense of self. This need is driven by a desire for recognition, acknowledgment, support, and affirmation and is one of the major factors in creating differences between siblings. While some children may try to establish their identity by imitating a sibling who is clearly affirmed and recognized by their parents, the more common pathway is to find something that will distinguish self from others.

Identical twins demonstrate the principle most clearly. Those who were separated at birth and raised in different families are more like each other in personality than those who are raised in the same family where they try to be different from each other.

The first child in a family usually identifies with the parents' values and works at becoming what they want. The second child (especially a second child of the same sex as the first) will most likely not be able to compete with the first one. He or she will therefore learn to open up new territory, try out new behaviors, and seek a different route for getting affirmation and recognition.

This can be a problem, however, if what the parents value most is reflected in the first child. The second child (especially of the same sex) may be seen as less "good" than the first — less competent at doing whatever it is that the parents value. Sometimes, when the first child is good at being "good" (i.e., fulfilling parental expectations), the second child gets his or her recognition by being good at being "bad."

Younger siblings tend to define themselves according to whatever territory has already been claimed by the older child. In therapy, two adult sisters began to explore this dynamic and the resentments between them that had resulted. May spoke of how much she envied the academic achievements of her older sister Alice, who clearly pleased her parents with her abilities. Quite early on, May decided she could not and would not compete with Alice in that area. She put more energy into friends, her social life, and team sports. She also became a cheerleader and eventually ended up becoming a television actress. It was news to her to hear how much Alice envied her. While they were growing up, May not only had a lot of dates, but seemed to Alice to be favored by dad since he appreciated and enjoyed her activities more than Alice's quiet work in the chemistry lab. As an adult, Alice wished she had the kind of public recognition May had.

d. SEX

Sex* adds another important dimension to birth order characteristics. Although all children who share the same birth position in their families will have some characteristics in common,

---

*Generally, in this book, the word sex refers to the biological fact of being male or female. Gender refers to the attributes of masculinity or femininity as defined by our culture.

they will differ according to their sex and the sex of others in their family.

Each succeeding child is treated by, and relates to, parents and siblings differently according to the sex of each of them. A boy born into a family of boys will see himself and, ultimately, the world in a different way from a boy born into a family of girls. This continues to be the case even in these days of increased equality for women and despite the professed belief of many parents in non-sexist childrearing.

Just about the first question the parents and everyone else asks about a newborn is "What is it?" They aren't asking if it's a puppy or a pony; they're asking what sex it is, in part so they know how to think of it and how to treat it. Research has shown that, from the moment of birth, girl infants are treated differently from boy infants. For instance, they are handled more gently and talked to more often. In one study, volunteers were asked to play with different infants. Each baby was first dressed as a boy and then as a girl. The volunteers thought there were two different babies each time, and they played with and talked to them in very different ways, according to the sex the babies were dressed as.

Sex is also a factor when the parents want a child of one sex and end up with the opposite. For example, in a family where a third girl is born to parents ardently wanting a boy, the impact on that girl's experience in the family and her sense of self can be very strong. The impact usually shows in one of two ways: she is either treated as a disappointment and ignored to some extent or is groomed to become the "boy" of the family.

And, of course, genetic research is increasing our understanding of biological differences between the sexes.

e. HOW SIBLINGS REACT TO EACH OTHER

Parents usually get the blame or credit for the way their children turn out. However, brothers and sisters in the family have a profound effect as well. Children — except for only children or oldest children for the first few years of life — develop in great measure by relating to their siblings and struggling to establish a separate identity within the family. By age five or six, this identity and the accompanying personality traits are more or less set. These early experiences in the family far outweigh the later influences of school, church, clubs, and friendships.

Birth order and sex are commonly used to identify a child. Parents will often introduce their children to outsiders by saying "This is my oldest," "This is my youngest son," "This is my only daughter." The child soon accepts these factors as part of his or her identity. What seems a superficial matter is important at a deep level of consciousness. In addition to whatever the parents believe about oldests, middles, and youngests, and about males and females, society's attitudes about these factors will also become part of the child's consciousness.

Almost all children learn to identify with their position and construct a story or form their own private beliefs about what it means to be a "first," a "middle," or a "last" child, or a "boy" or a "girl." Their stories, repeated to themselves daily in their heads, may have an essentially positive or negative tone, and as each day's events happen, only those elements that fit with the story will be noticed and remembered. It is not only the reality that makes the difference but the child's perception of reality that affects this identity.

Jeremy and his wife came into therapy partly because Jeremy didn't feel appreciated and loved by her. His negative feelings had increased substantially since their first child was born and the baby commanded so much of his wife's attention. Jeremy was asked if he had ever felt like that before. It came out that he had often felt his parents cared more for his younger brother, Wylie, than for him. He had never said anything about it to his parents, but had often been quiet and sulky at home, just as he was with his wife. Asked for a specific example of how his parents had favored Wylie, Jeremy told a story about being sent off to boarding school at a young age. He hated the school, was homesick, scared, and unhappy. A year later, Wylie came to the same school and had the same feelings about it. However,

Wylie immediately called his parents to say he wanted to come home. His parents came to the school to see him and encourage him. This happened several times during the year, and each time, Jeremy felt hurt that his parents were so concerned about Wylie. He interpreted this as their loving Wylie more.

Not long after Jeremy told this story, his parents came to visit from England. Jeremy was asked to bring them to a therapy session. In the session, the therapist asked them about their experience with their two sons. They both spoke about how much more responsible and competent Jeremy was than his younger brother Wylie. They said Wylie had always been a problem for them, but that Jeremy could be counted on. Asked for an example, they spontaneously told about sending both boys to boarding school. They never had a problem with Jeremy, who handled it just fine, they said, but Wylie complained constantly and kept dragging them down to the school to deal with his problems. They tried to be understanding, but inside they wished Wylie could handle it like Jeremy. To this day, Wylie came to them with his complaints and pleas for help.

Tears filled Jeremy's eyes as he listened to this version of the story. He had never seen it from this perspective. When he told his father that he had been just as upset by his first year at school as Wylie, his father said he'd never known that. It began to emerge that Jeremy thought people who loved him (including his wife) should just know what he felt and needed. He had never asked for what he wanted directly, but just sulked quietly instead. As a result, his perception of situations became the reality for him and that "reality" shaped his responses.

Children often learn to use their birth order position to advantage to get what they want. In reaction to each other, they reinforce each other's characteristics. A youngest child like Wylie may decide to excel in using relative weakness to get attention from the parents; an oldest child like Jeremy may be pushed to even greater efforts to excel at some accomplishment in order to get affirmation from the parents.

At one level, Jeremy understood that his parents valued his quieter, less demanding style, but that created a bind for him because it prevented him from getting the attention he wanted. He achieved some recognition by being more adult, but some of his emotional needs were not met.

Because all members of a family define themselves in relation to other family members, a change in any one family member always has an impact on every other family member.

This process is especially true for siblings. Any one child's behavior and way of expressing self in the world has to be seen in the context of the other children. They don't make each other the way they are; but they all define themselves in the context of their relationship with each other.

Arthur frequently had physical fights with his older brother, which he usually lost. He craved his older brother's attention, respect, and acceptance. But the older brother preferred to be with the third, youngest boy who was a more compliant companion. Arthur's father seemed to dote on the oldest son, and his mother spent her time with his sisters. He felt like an outsider. Early in adolescence, after years of trying to be like his older brother and failing miserably, Arthur began to avoid the family. He became a loner, saying he didn't need them or anybody.

After getting married, Arthur became intensely attached to his wife. He was sensitive to her every emotional move toward or away from him. Their relationship worked pretty well until they had children. With each child he became more jealous and more demanding of his wife's attention. His wife complained that he was just too demanding and wanted to control her. They were on the verge of separating when they tried therapy. Once his experience in his family was explored, both Arthur and his wife were relieved to see how this was a major factor in his life and the way he experienced his marriage. He was trying to make up for his loneliness in the family through his marriage.

Arthur began to sort through his family issues, inviting his brothers, sisters, and parents into his therapy at different times. His major task, however, was to begin to define himself in ways that did not depend on his perception of how others responded to him. He needed to focus more on what made sense to him about how to be, rather than on how he thought he had to be in order to be connected with others. As he did this, he found he got into fewer upsetting situations. His life calmed down and became more satisfying, and he established a better relationship with all his family members. "I have my family back," he said.

f.   ONGOING EFFECTS OF BIRTH ORDER

Sigmund Freud was the first of the psychotherapists to note that "a child's position in the sequence of brothers and sisters is of very great significance for the course of his later life."

Your birth order and sex determine in large part how other people in your family react to you and treat you. That, in turn, influences what you think about yourself and how you react to and treat others inside and outside the family.

Your family is your classroom for learning how to behave in the world. In the family, you learn how males and females act; how youngest or oldest children act; how different sexes and ages relate to each other. Whether or not it was an enjoyable lesson a happy home for you, you usually learn your role so well (and so unconsciously) that you live it out the rest of your life without even knowing you've been in "school."

Pioneer psychologist Alfred Adler said, "It should not surprise us to learn that people do not change their attitude toward life after their infancy, though its expressions in later life are quite different from those of their earliest days."

The family experience is so powerful in your early life that you may grow up with the firm conviction (which again may be unconscious) that the way things are in your family is as natural as water to a fish and that anything else is deviant. It is, for example, why you may think the normal way to squeeze the toothpaste tube is from the middle and your spouse is equally convinced it is from the bottom, and neither of you can understand how the other could possibly do it differently.

"The little world of childhood with its familiar surroundings is a model of the greater world," said Carl Jung. "The more intensively the family has stamped its character upon the child, the more it will tend to feel and see its earlier miniature world again in the bigger world of adult life. Naturally this is not a conscious, intellectual process."

This conviction that your way is the right way exists even if you consciously dislike your family of origin (the family one is born and raised in) and the way you were brought up. You may not like it, but it is what you are used to. One result of this may be that you will try to duplicate early family experiences, even painful ones, in other areas of your life.

Take, for example, the woman who comes from a family where either she or her mother was abused by her father and who ends up being abused in her marriage. She didn't "look for" this kind of man (and certainly didn't want to be abused), but since that was the kind of man she was accustomed to, he was the kind of man she felt "at home" with when she first met him.

Your experiences at home will also affect your expectations and judgments of situations and relationships. You will react to many of the events in the rest of your life the same way you reacted to them in your family. This can sometimes be dangerous.

For instance, you may assume people or events are duplicating the ones you knew as a child when they're not like that at all. The younger son whose mother and big sister were overprotective and possessive may react resentfully when his wife asks him how his day was. He is so accustomed to women being "domineering" and "snoopy" (according to his perception of his family) that he is automatically angered by an innocent remark. The middle manager who thinks an ambitious young co-worker is trying to undermine her work to win the top boss's favor may react the same way she did to her younger sister trying to win favor with father. In both cases, the reaction, which is to old hurts, may be inappropriate in the current context and destructive to everyone involved.

It is important, then, to be aware of how your position in your family and your early experiences have shaped you and your relationships with others. Murray Bowen, one of the originators of family systems therapy, often tells therapists that "no single piece of data is more important than knowing the sibling positions of people in the present and past generations."

g. PURPOSE OF THIS BOOK

This book will help you answer, in part, the question "Why am I like this?" The summary of research findings about birth order positions in a family should help you recognize aspects of your own personality and understand their origin.

While it may be comforting to find out that some of your less desirable characteristics were almost inevitable given your sex and birth order, it isn't helpful to blame your faults on that and give up trying to change. The point of knowing how those characteristics developed is to learn strategies for changing the ones you don't like. Just because you were born as a youngest or an oldest or an only, you do not have to keep on behaving like one; the traits are not written in stone.

Many of the descriptions in this book are not very flattering. It almost seems that there is no "good" birth order. Each of the birth order positions has characteristics that are helpful and make life easier for the person, and each presents challenges to face.

These descriptions of the birth order positions for each sex report what most people in these positions are usually like according to research studies; they do not say what anyone should be like. They are descriptive, not prescriptive. They simply provide one more framework for looking at yourself and your relationships. (See the appendix for more details on the research.) The most valuable and extensive research has been done by Austrian psychologist Walter Toman, whose book *Family Constellation: Its Effect on Personality and Social Behavior* (Springer, 1976) is a classic in the field and is highly recommended for your further reading.

For many reasons, some of which are discussed in chapter 15, the description of your birth order may not fit you at all. It may seem about as meaningful as a horoscope reading or a fortune cookie. If this is your experience, first ask someone who knows you well to read the description of your birth order position and see if it fits. We are not always the best judges of our own character. If your outside reader agrees that the description does not fit, you may be interested in finding out why this is so. What aspects of your family situation have affected the development of the usual birth order characteristics?

h. USING THE INFORMATION

The best way to use the information in this book is to see how your birth order may have led you to think and behave in certain ways. If those ways are working well for you, this can be just an interesting intellectual exercise. If some of the ways you think and act are causing problems for you or others in your life, you may want to use this information as a springboard for making some changes. Since people are most often motivated to make changes when they are dissatisfied, the birth order descriptions here focus on the more troublesome aspects of each birth order position rather than the more positive ones. It's the troublesome aspects that you will want to deal with in some way; the good times can just keep rolling.

The information about birth order characteristics can also help you understand why others in your life think and behave as they do. It can be very constructive for you to understand that a person's way of being with you may be related to these standard birth order characteristics and is not just deliberate perverseness on their part. You may be able to accept someone's behavior more easily when you can say to yourself, "Well, that's just how oldest brothers of brothers are. He's like that with everybody; it's not that he dislikes me." The next chapter describes some of the ways birth order can affect different kinds of relationships.

Be sure you read only with the intent of using the information to discover how you might want to change in relating to others. It would be a misuse of this information to start labeling those around you as a "such and such" as a way of putting them down or trying to get them to change. As always, in attempts at self-improvement, remember that it's not self-improvement if you're trying to improve someone else. It's difficult enough to change your own behavior; it's impossible to impose change on someone else. However, if you change the way you act with someone, eventually that person may change in response to your change.

Many therapists prefer to work with the "healthiest" person in a relationship, the one who would appear to need changing the least, because that person has the best chance of successfully making changes. Changes on the part of one person usually alter the way a relationship functions. But don't make that the goal of your change. Your only goal for change can be for yourself and how you treat others.

Understanding birth order characteristics precedes change, but doesn't decree change. Knowing that some of your traits are common among people in your birth order position may simply help you see why you feel like a square peg trying to fit into a round hole. You can then decide whether you want to work on being rounder or whether you want to find a squarer hole to fit into.

Elsie, an oldest sister of sisters, had become a secretary because that was the only kind of work open to her as a young woman 30 years ago. She had good skills and good work habits, yet she had been dissatisfied in most of her jobs. She had little respect for the men and women she worked for (especially the women), was unable to be supportive of her bosses, and lost several jobs because of her "attitude." When she learned about birth order characteristics, it began to make sense that she wouldn't adapt well to the traditional subordinate role of a secretary. Learning that the fit wasn't right for her motivated her to look seriously at other kinds of work where her birth order characteristics would be an asset rather than a hindrance.

Elsie might also have made the decision to pay particular attention to those aspects of her birth order characteristics that caused her problems at work and to be aware of when she was acting like an oldest sister rather than a professional secretary. She could then have consciously made the effort not to think of her boss as a younger sister who needed straightening out.

We hope that by learning a little bit about the usual characteristics for your sex and birth order, you will better understand and accept yourself and others in your life. Chapter 17 provides a worksheet for using this information in a constructive way to change those aspects of your functioning that are hindering you in some way.

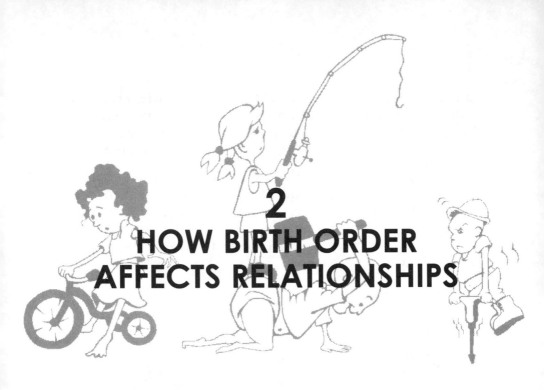

2
HOW BIRTH ORDER
AFFECTS RELATIONSHIPS

*All marriages are happy. It's the living together after-
ward that causes all the trouble.*

Raymond Hill

Your birth order and gender affect primarily your social behavior — how you relate to other people in your life. They affect the kind of spouse you are, the kind of parent you are, the kind of employer or employee you are, and the kind of friend you are. Some people, because of their gender and birth order, will have more trouble than others at work, some will have more difficulty being a parent, and some will have more conflict in their relationships with the opposite sex. This is good to be aware of, especially when deciding on a career, choosing a mate, having a child, or working on difficulties you may be having in these areas.

You learn early how to be a social being. A newborn develops a relationship first with parents and then with siblings. The way the child learns to relate to these significant people sets the pattern for how the adult will relate to other significant people in life.

The overall tenor of the family sets the framework. A family with a basically optimistic or benign approach to life provides a different framework for the children than that of a family with a hostile or angry approach to life. The oldest child in an easy-going, fun-loving family is likely to be the most serious, responsible child in that family, but a much looser, happier person than an oldest child in a rigid, serious family. The youngest child in both those families is likely to be less responsible and more helpless, but the one from the happy family will be more playful and carefree, while the one from the serious family may be quiet or even depressed.

Within the family framework, too, children can create very different pictures for themselves as shown by Jeremy and Wylie in chapter 1. Birth order is one of the lenses through which children develop a view of themselves and the world, and create their story or identity.

a. YOUR SPOUSE

The term "spouse" here includes legal and common-law spouses and the partners in other live-in love relationships. Gay partners can extrapolate somewhat from the information, but keep in mind that the research in this area is extremely sparse. However, anecdotal evidence from gay couples in therapy indicates that the relationship patterns are similar to those of heterosexual couples.

Living with someone in an intimate relationship is the situation that most nearly duplicates the experience of growing up in a family. It is hardly surprising, then, that birth order characteristics usually become most evident and even accentuated in relating to a spouse. Jeremy's way of relating emotionally to his wife was much the same way he related in his family, and he experienced his child as he had his younger brother.

Of course, many things affect the nature of your love relationships. The way your parents related to each other is your basic model for such relationships. The quality and tone is usually similar, though not necessarily the content. For example, you may argue about different things with your spouse, but your preferred style of arguing may be similar to the way your parents argued and your spouse's style similar to his or her parents' way. The differences or similarities between your cultural backgrounds, ages, educational levels, and values will also affect how well you can live with one another over the long term.

However, your relationship will also reflect the way people in your birth order positions usually get along. The combination of your birth order and your spouse's birth order will have some effect on your relationship. Other things being equal, some matches work better than others simply because the birth orders are well matched. Being well matched in this case usually means most nearly duplicating the age and sex arrangement that you each were used to as children. You already know how to act and what to expect if your spouse has the same sibling position as your opposite-sex sibling. For example, the youngest sister of a brother is usually well matched with an oldest brother of a sister. Both are used to that particular relationship of sex and relative age, and "know how to act" with each other. In effect, the spouse takes the place of the sibling. Their positions are complementary. The better their family experience has been, the better the current relationship will feel and function.

Even those who didn't "like" their sibling while growing up are still on familiar ground and may be more comfortable with this arrangement than with a spouse whose sibling position is the opposite. For instance, a woman who had an older brother who was always in charge, protective, and caring may expect her spouse to be like this. If her spouse is a younger brother, he may not meet this expectation. This could lead her to feel abandoned and unloved.

Complementary relationships can become difficult if one spouse wants to change. The younger sister married to an older brother may eventually want to be more independent and then start resenting her husband's natural tendency to take charge of things or take care of her. He may resist her attempts to "grow up" in the same way he tried to keep his younger siblings from trying to usurp his position. But even in this case, the battleground may be familiar and earlier adaptations helpful in the new situation.

On the other hand, if you are in a situation that is quite different from what you were familiar with as a child, you will have more difficulty coping with it. A case in point might be the relationship of an oldest sister of sisters married to an oldest brother of brothers. They are both used to being the eldest and therefore the "authority," and neither is used to family peers of the opposite sex. They are more likely than other matches to have conflict over both control and lack of understanding of the other sex.

Although the best match may often be the one that most closely duplicates the family of origin arrangement, it isn't always the one that people seek. We are often attracted at first to people who have many things in common with us. Thus, two oldest children may be able to sympathize with each other and share their common frustrations and burdens. They may think they have found a kindred spirit. It's only after living together for a while that they find their spirits may be kindred, but their personalities are in constant conflict over who is boss of the household.

Another thing that sometimes prevents people from choosing the mate who is likely to be most compatible is the conscious or unconscious effort to find someone totally different from a sibling. If there has been much conflict between siblings, a mate who bears no resemblance to the sibling may seem most desirable. What isn't apparent is that even though there may have been conflict, the siblings have at least learned how to deal with that kind of conflict. They won't have a clue about how to deal with conflict when it involves someone from a non-complementary birth position.

On the other hand, if you have felt especially close to a sibling, you may unconsciously have some fears about incestuous relationships and thus look for someone who is nothing like the favored sibling. Again, you may end up disappointed by the reality of living with someone whose birth position is in conflict with your own instead of similar to what you knew at home.

For most people, of course, it is too late to look for a spouse of complementary birth order. The choice has been made. If it is one of the theoretically "poorer" matches, it doesn't mean there is no hope; it simply means you have to work harder to overcome that particular handicap. Being aware of this potential source of friction in a non-complementary relationship can make the problems more manageable.

It is useful to know that something as simple as birth order can account for major conflicts in a relationship and that neither person is to "blame." It is just that the differences between you are more challenging than most to live with. Once you understand, for example, that an oldest brother of brothers and an oldest sister of sisters married to each other are bound to have conflicts over who is in charge, you can stop blaming each other and accept the fact that it is a difficult combination. You may, perhaps, even learn to laugh at your conflicts as you catch yourselves acting like a typical oldest sister of sisters or oldest brother of brothers.

b. YOUR FRIENDS

Friendships are also affected by birth order. The friends you get along well with are likely to be in a complementary birth position. Non-complementary birth positions may partly explain any tension that exists in a friendship. Differences of opinion that may appear to be the result of rational thinking may simply reflect early family experiences.

Annette and Sue were neighbors, and they enjoyed each other's company, shared the same interest in local politics, and had children the same age. However, they often had strong disagreements about a variety of issues, especially the subject of men in general and their own spouses in particular. Sue always defended the actions of men, made excuses for her husband's poor treatment of her, and was critical of feminists. Annette thought Sue's husband treated her intolerably and couldn't understand why Sue put up with him. It was no surprise to learn that Sue was the oldest sister of a brother (and therefore used to taking care of men and making excuses for their childish behavior) and Annette was an only child (and most interested in her own and other women's rights).

If you take note of the kind of relationship you have with various friends and then find out their birth order, you may find that your best friends all have the same birth order. While you may have much in common with people in your same birth order, over the long haul you will probably feel most comfortable with friends from a complementary birth order, especially one that matches that of a favorite sibling.

Manny, an only child, found that he was usually most uncomfortable with friends, male or female, who were oldests. He couldn't tolerate being with people who wanted to be in charge or who thought they knew best. However, he was also leery of youngests who expected him to be in charge or take care of them. He enjoyed "playing" with the youngests, and liked it when they looked up to him, but would disappear as soon as they indicated he should do something to make life better for them. "Do it yourself" was his attitude. As with many only children, he was his own best friend.

c. YOUR PARENTS

Your parents, of course, are the most powerful influence in your life. They shape your world, as theirs was shaped by their parents. Their influence is diluted only by the fact that they are so much older than you, which is why your siblings and your sex and birth order become so important.

But your parents and the way they were treated as children, their own birth order, and the way they treat each other still have a tremendous impact on your personality development.

1. The effect of birth order — theirs and yours

Your parents' birth orders may partly explain why they treated you as they did. Birth order affects the kind of parent a person tends to be. People in the different birth order positions have different skills and shortcomings as parents.

Larry had always felt neglected by his parents and frustrated by the daily chaos in his home. Then he learned that his parents were both the babies in their families. When he realized what that usually means in terms of parenting skills — since a youngest rarely has any experience taking care of others — he was more understanding about their difficulty in nurturing or disciplining him, and more appreciative of the spontaneous fun he had with each of them. He also understood why they each always expected the other to take responsibility and neither of them would. Finding out that their apparent neglect had little to do with him as a person or his parents' love for him helped Larry develop a much more rewarding relationship with them in their old age.

Birth order also explains why parents may treat each of their children differently. Their own birth order can affect what they think of — and therefore how they raise — each of their children. They may react to you the way they reacted to their own siblings in the same birth order position. They may be trying to avoid the past or to duplicate it.

Bernie was an oldest brother of a brother. He had spent most of his life taking care of and rescuing his brother who was an alcoholic. When Bernie had three children of his own (girl, boy, girl), his son replaced his brother as a focus of concern. The experience with his brother made Bernie anxious over the simplest problems his son encountered and prompted Bernie to play his familiar role of rescuing the younger male. The son reacted to dad's rescuing behavior by taking less and less responsibility for himself. Eventually, he too became an alcoholic and died of an alcohol overdose at the age of 36. Bernie did not "make" his son into an alcoholic — another son in a similar situation might have reacted differently, but Bernie's sibling experience had set him up for a repeat performance.

The way you relate to your parents can also be affected by a complementary or non-complementary birth order. If your birth order is complementary to one or both of your parents (you are in the same position as a sibling of theirs), you may have a more comfortable fit between you. For example, if you are the youngest brother of brothers and your father is the oldest brother of brothers, you may have a close, or at least easy, relationship with your father because you will have some of the same traits as his familiar younger brother. However, if you are the oldest sister of sisters, your oldest-brother-of-brothers father may find it more difficult to relate to you (and you to him), as both your sex and your birth position will be in conflict with him.

If your parent had a difficult time with his or her siblings, your complementary position could be a disadvantage for you. If you are the oldest sister of sisters and your mother was a youngest sister of sisters, she may not relate well to your serious side or your need for high achievement. If she perceives you as being domineering like her older sister was, she may empathize with your younger sister and take her side in any disputes.

Parents who have the same birth order as a child of theirs often understand that child better than the others, but may have more conflicts as they clash head-on in assuming that particular role in the family.

Ed was an oldest who worked hard at impressing his father with his accomplishments. Dad was an oldest, too, and was proud of his son, but found it difficult to spend much time with him. They often argued about the best way to do something. Dad was often disappointed in Ed's younger brother Mickey, but spent more time playing ball with him than he had with Ed. Ed's mother, a youngest, was less impressed with Ed's accomplishments and wished he had a better social life, but she felt more comfortable with him than with Mickey.

Knowing how birth order affects personalities and relationships is helpful in understanding why your parents and their siblings and their own parents relate to each other in certain ways. For example, if you are the youngest sister of sisters, you may have a wonderful relationship with your oldest-sister-of-sisters grandmother and be bewildered at the enmity between her and your father who is an oldest brother of sisters. It could be that their non-complementary positions make it difficult for them to understand each other.

If your birth order is neither the same as nor complementary to either of your parent's, you may feel somewhat isolated in your family. You could be a birth order "misfit" in their experience, which might make it difficult for your parents to know how to relate to you. For example, if you are the youngest brother of brothers and both your parents are the oldest siblings of sisters, neither has had a younger brother and neither knows what it's like to be a youngest.

2. Learning to relate to the opposite sex

The way you relate as an adult to the opposite sex is influenced in part by your relationship with your opposite-sex parent. And that relationship is affected to some degree by your parent's birth order.

The oldest brother of brothers, for example, may have more conflict with a mother who is the oldest sister of sisters than he would with a mother who was the youngest sister of brothers. The conflict in his relationship with his mother may make it even more difficult for him to relate well to other women in his life.

Your opposite-sex parent's birth order has the most influence on you when your siblings are the same sex as you. In this situation, your parent is the chief clue you have about relating to the opposite sex. The quality of your relationship is likely to be repeated in your other relationships with the opposite sex. For example, if you have no brothers and your father is the youngest of four brothers, you may grow up seeing men as slightly childish, playful, and maybe irresponsible, with little understanding of women. This perception is likely to affect your approach to other males in your life. If, however, you have an older brother who is a high achiever and very responsible, this will color your picture of what men are like.

While your same-sex parent acts as a role model for how you behave as a male or a female, your opposite-sex parent has a greater influence on your self-image. Thus, a mother who is the youngest sister of a brother may be more admiring and supportive of her son and his maleness than an oldest-sister-of-sisters mother who has little understanding of men and little respect for "juniors."

d. YOUR CHILDREN

As the above section indicates, your birth order can affect the kind of parent you are and the kind of relationship you have with each of your children, just as your child's birth order will affect how he or she sees you.

If you are an oldest or a middle child, you probably either had some experience caring for younger children or witnessed it. Parenthood may come easily to you and be most fulfilling. You may be inclined to take too much responsibility for or be too controlling with your children; however, you may simply be a good and nurturing caretaker.

If you are an only child or a youngest child, you haven't had the chance to do or observe any parenting other than what you received, and you may feel overwhelmed by the responsibility "of being a parent" and unsure about how to do it. On the other hand, you are likely to be less overpowering as a parent than an oldest and able, by default, to allow your children quite a bit of autonomy. If you are a youngest, you may enjoy playing with your children more than most parents do.

Helena and Gina were sisters. They grew up together in a small town in Vermont, went to the same schools, and had the same extended family around them. They both married local boys, and they both became single mothers of male only children due to losing their husbands in the war. But the similarities ended there. Helena was five years older than Gina. She had never been in trouble, had always been "responsible," and had always done what was expected of her. Young Gina was the "rebel" and rarely did what she was supposed to do. As a result, Helena and Gina became very different kinds of parents to their sons. After her husband's death, Helena never married again or even dated other men. She took her parenting duties very seriously and was highly protective of her son Jeff. She did everything she thought a good parent should do. She stayed in their large family home for Jeff's sake. She always took him to Sunday School. She did everything for him at home, and when he had a problem out in the world she stepped in to make sure it was dealt with correctly. He lived with many rules and was kept close to home and to his mother for all his growing up years. He had very little private life.

As an adult, Jeff dated quite a bit, but he "never found the right woman." Any of his more serious relationships tended to be with women much older than himself. He did not develop a career direction of his own and went from job to job, with long periods of not working in between. At the age of 40 he was still living at home with Helena.

Gina dearly loved her son Adam, but did little "for him" other than providing a fairly stable home life. Like her older sister she also worked full time while her son was growing up. After her husband's death, Gina started dating again and remarried once while Adam was young but got divorced after six months. She decided that she liked dating more than she liked marriage.

She and Adam moved often from apartment to apartment and lived together almost like roommates. While she did exercise some discipline and control over him in his earlier years, by the time he was in seventh grade, they each had their own lives and came and went almost as they pleased. During his adolescence, they barely saw each other. She never asked him about his day or what he was doing. There was a lot of potential for him to get into trouble, but he never did. He was a happy, even-tempered, "good kid." He got married after finishing college and moved to Boston to begin a career in advertising.

One Christmas, when the two cousins were in their forties, it was decided to have a small family reunion at Helena and Jeff's home. Adam and his wife and two children and Gina timed their flights from two different cities so they could all be met at the airport by Jeff. On the drive to the house, they went by a bar, which Jeff pointed out, saying "That's where I went when I was first allowed to stay out after midnight." Adam asked his cousin how old he was when this happened. Jeff said, "Nineteen." Turning to his mother in the back seat, Adam said, "You know, I don't ever remember you telling me a time I had to be home by." Gina said, "That's right. I didn't have to. You were always home before me."

Helena's parenting style was typical of oldest siblings who tend to take more responsibility and be more involved with their children. Gina's style was a more extreme example of how youngests may opt out of the traditional parenting role. As you can see from the results, the birth-order inspired parenting style is not a predictor of how the child will turn out.

In addition to parenting characteristics related to your particular birth order, you may react to one or more of your children out of old patterns of behavior developed in relation to your own siblings. You may favor the child who shares your sex and birth order position, having sympathy and understanding for his or her familiar struggles. Or you may have conflict over the roles if, for example, you are an oldest and you and your oldest child struggle over who is in charge of the younger children. Of course, as an adult, you are in a better position to modify your behavior with your children than you were as a child with your siblings or parents.

Your relationship with a favored sibling while you are growing up may also affect your relationship with your child who is the same birth order and sex as that sibling. You may enjoy that child most as a companion while having the same kind of disagreements you had with your sibling.

Be aware, too, of how a child of yours might remind you of a sibling. Take note of your responses to certain behaviors. Otherwise unexplainable negative reactions to a child may actually reflect an earlier struggle with a sibling. Are your feelings relevant to the situation today or are they a throwback to confrontations of yesterday?

If you are able to be aware of and change, if necessary, the way you relate to your own siblings and parents as a result of your birth order, you will have a better chance of also changing the way you relate to your children.

Sometimes each parent favors a different child, particularly in two-child families where each parent unconsciously takes one child for himself or herself. This is a danger when it creates parent/child allies rather than parent/parent allies.

Chapter 16 discusses in more detail how to use the information about birth order characteristics in your parenting.

e. YOUR ADULT SIBLINGS

Most of this book is about the relationships between siblings as children and how that affects your later relationships with others. How you relate to your siblings as adults is one of those later relationships. Chapter 17 goes into greater detail about how to use your current relationship with siblings as a resource in your own growth. For now, it's only necessary to mention that it's not unusual for childhood patterns to continue well into adulthood.

If your parents obviously favored one of their children over the others, that child may be resented and disliked by the others even as an adult. Some siblings continue fighting for the favor of their parents all their lives — even after the parents have died.

If you and a sibling were close together in age, you were more likely to have conflicts than if further apart in years, and those conflicts probably still exist. It may not have been possible to admit those conflicts openly or to deal with them as a child, so they may be hidden, yet still control the way you relate.

Siblings with a greater age gap between them often have fewer, but more openly acknowledged conflicts. Being more aware of the conflicts usually enables those siblings to deal with them and get over them. You are more likely to have fewer conflicts and a closer relationship with a sibling much older or much younger than you.

As you and your siblings get older and more settled and established in your own lives, the minor rivalries and competition from childhood are likely to recede. As older, more relaxed adults you may be able to enjoy sharing your memories and telling the different versions of your growing-up stories.

By learning about the pressures and difficulties facing each of you in your birth order positions, you can better understand why you reacted to each other as you did in childhood. When you see that your "privileged" older sister was undergoing her own sufferings from all the pressure on her, you may feel less angry about the way she bossed you around. When you see that your "spoiled" younger sister felt helpless and inadequate in relation to you, you may feel less resentful of her "easy life."

f. PEOPLE AT WORK

The kind of job you have or the level of career you pursue is determined to great extent by family background — what resources were available, the family's expectations and attitude toward education and success, the options and opportunities available to you. But within that range, how well you fit into your role, how you function in your job, how you relate to co-workers, and how you do things such as give and receive supervision is influenced by your birth order.

President Lyndon Johnson developed his style of leadership as the oldest brother of three sisters and a brother. When given chores to do, he assigned them to his siblings. "He was a hard taskmaster with them.... If the younger children didn't do the chores, they weren't done, for Lyndon wouldn't do them," writes biographer Robert Caro.

Work situations often seem quite similar to family situations, but without the safety net of being bonded by blood and having at least the ideal of, if not actual, love between individuals. Since people who work outside the home spend half their waking hours in that setting, these work relationships can be a significant factor in determining life satisfaction.

Your boss may unknowingly fit emotionally into the role of one of your parents and your co-workers into the role of siblings, for good or for ill. You could have complementary relationships that make you a good working team or you could have non-complementary relationships that pit you against each other. You might react to these people, especially in times of stress, in the same way you reacted as a child to parents or siblings, without realizing where your inappropriate fear or anger comes from.

Gordon worked as a production manager for a large printing company. His boss wrote an article for the company newsletter announcing Gordon's recent promotion. Gordon was furious about the article. He thought the article sounded as if it was about the boss's abilities as a supervisor rather than about Gordon's good work. When exploring this unexpected reaction later in therapy, Gordon was asked what his feelings reminded him of. He immediately recalled how he had often reacted the same way to his older brother. He had thought, as a child, that everything his brother did in relation to him was designed to put the brother in a better light and deflect Gordon's credit to him. Even though his boss had praised him in the newsletter, Gordon's old suspicions took over.

As a boss, the way you treat your employees may also reflect your experiences in your sibling position. An oldest brother of brothers who took charge of the younger boys in his family may be loath to give much responsibility to employees and may resent any questioning of his authority or attempts by others to get ahead. As the employee of this man, you may chafe more under his thumb if he resembles your own older brother and reminds you of your futile attempts to win your parents' praise.

An oldest-brother boss who was a guide and mentor to his younger brothers may be eager to help a younger man get ahead. He may also think women have no place in management and subvert any attempt on the part of female employees to advance in their careers. The younger sister of a brother may be less inclined to fight against such a boss than an oldest sister who may either wonder what is wrong with her that she is not getting ahead or confront her boss with her lack of progress.

A male only child may expect to have the same attention, privileges, and advantages as an employee that he had as a child. The discovery that he is expected to fit into a different and less comfortable mold than he is accustomed to may come as a rude shock.

Knowing how birth order characteristics affect work relationships can help you be better prepared for what you might expect from yourself and others. You will probably find that you work best with or for some birth orders than others. You may also realize that you prefer people from certain birth orders as employees.

Gerard, an only child, had had a series of executive assistants who just didn't live up to his expectations. They were capable women, but he kept being disappointed that they didn't take on more responsibility for running his busy office and didn't work hard enough. Then he hired someone who turned out to be highly capable and also eager to take on more responsibility and do much of his work for him, which he appreciated. He couldn't figure out what had changed in his approach to hiring until he found out, after the fact, that all the previous assistants had been youngest sisters of brothers (as was his mother), who were charming and clever, but not the workhorses he needed. His current assistant was the oldest sister of brothers and sisters and very willing to run things and give the credit to Gerard.

Keep in mind, however, that it is probably illegal to discriminate in hiring on the basis of birth order, even though it's not officially on the list of questions you're prohibited from asking in job interviews!

3
FINDING THE DESCRIPTION OF YOUR SEX AND BIRTH ORDER POSITION

*Till one can see the "family" in oneself, one can see nei-
ther oneself or any other family clearly.*

R. D. Laing, *Self and Others*

The characteristics described in the following chapters of this
book seem to be generally representative of average middle-
class North Americans and Europeans of each sex in each of the
birth order positions. Few people exhibit all the characteristics
of their sex and birth order position, but most people will recognize at least some aspect of themselves in these descriptions.
Where there is great variation from the expected characteristics,
it is often because of other more powerful influences in the family that have interrupted in some way the usual patterns of development (see chapter 15 for more information about factors
that create exceptions to the rule).

However, the descriptions should come close to reflecting your basic personality and approach to life. The one thing that is absolutely certain is that if you were born in a different order and of a different sex, you would have characteristics very different from those you now have.

a. CIRCUMSTANCES OF BIRTH

All other things being equal, birth order traits develop on the basis of five circumstances of birth:

(a) The order of birth, whether first child, second child, last child, etc.

(b) The sex of the child

(c) The number of years between the births of siblings

(d) The sex of the siblings

(e) To a lesser degree, the birth order of the parents, particularly the same-sex parent

All the major birth order positions for each sex are described here. An almost infinite number of other variations exists, depending on the number of siblings, their sex, and their relative ages. However, all the sibling positions are some combination of those presented here. By doing some mixing and matching, you can figure out the description for your own particular birth order.

1. Order of birth

The major divisions discussed here are oldest, youngest, and middle children, only children, and twins. General descriptions are given first for each of these ordinal positions, and then each position is discussed according to sex.

The characteristics of middle children are the most difficult to pin down and require the most interpretation in reading the descriptions. For example, if you are a middle child, you should begin by reading the general chapter on middle children. Then, if you are the middle brother of brothers, you should read the description of the oldest brother of brothers plus the one for the youngest brother of brothers because you will share some characteristics with each of them.

The special characteristics of twins are described in the chapter on twins, but twins are also either oldests, youngests, or middle siblings in relation to the rest of the family so you should read whichever of those chapters is relevant as well.

2.   Sex

Sex counts — not so much because of biology as because of sociology. Girls and boys are treated differently in our society by everyone from the delivery nurse to grade school teachers and employers. While oldest girls and boys have many things in common, they are also different in many ways because of their sex and the gender characteristics that they pick up from the society around them. So, for example, if you are an oldest female, you should look at the chapter on oldests in general and then the chapter on oldest sisters.

3.   Number of years between siblings

The smaller the age difference between siblings, the more influence they usually have on each other. A middle child who is closer in age to the oldest child usually develops more youngest child characteristics than oldest child characteristics in relation to the youngest child. However, if that middle child became the primary caretaker of the younger sibling, and spent a great deal of time with him or her, then the middle child would have more characteristics of an oldest.

If there are more than five or six years between siblings, each will have many of the characteristics of an only child in addition to the characteristics of his or her own birth order. For example, Alfred Hitchcock was the youngest in his family but he followed his sister by seven years, so he developed many attributes of an only child. He was alone often and "more given to observation than participation," says biographer John Russell

Taylor. "He invented for himself games with ship routes...planning imaginary journeys, always by himself, for he recalls no playmate to share his childish enthusiasms." Similarly, the oldest sister of a brother seven years younger is most like an only child (which she was for seven years), but also has some of the traits of an oldest sister of brothers.

When there are large age gaps between groups of siblings, sub-groups will form, with those in each sub-group developing the characteristics of the position they occupy within that group. For example, in a family where there are three female children, then a gap of six years followed by two males two years apart, the oldest male will usually be more like an oldest brother of brothers than like a younger brother of sisters. The greater the age gap is, the more this is true. However, the characteristics of an oldest of a sub-group are seldom as pronounced as those of the true oldest child in that family.

4. Sex of the siblings

The way you relate to your siblings depends not only on your sex, but theirs too. For instance, there is usually more jealousy between two brothers than between a brother and a sister. The chapters on oldest sisters and oldest brothers and youngest sisters and youngest brothers are subdivided further according to the sex of the siblings. So, if you are an oldest brother of brothers, you should read that section as well as the general chapter on oldests. If you have both younger brothers and sisters, you will have some characteristics of an oldest brother of brothers and some of an oldest brother of sisters, so you should read both those sections as well as the section on oldest brothers of brothers and sisters.

Usually the sibling closest in age to you will have the most impact on you, so if you are an oldest sister followed by a brother, then a sister, you will probably be closer in personality to the oldest sister of brothers than to the oldest sister of sisters, though you will have some characteristics of that position as well. However, if your brother, at age six, was sent to boarding school, then you probably developed more characteristics of an oldest sister of sisters.

It also makes a difference when all the siblings are the same sex. For instance, one study of 25 highly successful business women found that all of them were either oldests or onlies, and that none of the oldests had brothers. This indicates that when there are no boys, the parents' ambitions are focused on the oldest female. However, in families where a boy is born later, it is not at all unusual for this oldest female to be supplanted.

5.   Birth order of the same-sex parent

Because most children emulate to some degree their same-sex parent, that parent's birth order is also a factor. Even if you consciously try as an adult not to be like your same-sex parent (the "I'll never treat my kids like that" syndrome), some of those characteristics will be embedded in your personality. It's easier to ferret them out when you know what your same-sex parent's birth order is and what traits are commonly associated with that birth order.

In talking with his new wife about child-raising philosophies, only child Jorgi said he never wanted to be the kind of father his father (a youngest) was. He provided little guidance or nurture for Jorgi. However, after they had children, Jorgi found he had little tolerance for the children's constant demands. Though he felt loving toward them, he did not know how to behave with them and found himself avoiding them much as his father avoided him.

Those who have siblings of both sexes are more likely than others to be influenced by the sibling position of the same-sex parent, particularly if that parent's position is the same as one of the positions of the child. For example, if you are a youngest brother of brothers and sisters and your father is a youngest brother of sisters, you will probably have more of the traits of a youngest brother of sisters than of brothers.

If you and your same-sex parent are the same birth order, you are likely to have more of the characteristics of that birth order as described here than if your parent is a different birth order.

Stewart was the middle of three boys as was his father. His personality was much like his father's, and he had the same kind of uneasy relationship with his older brother that his father had with his older brother. Stewart's mother often said to him, "You're more like your father than he is." Because Stewart saw the problems that his father and uncle had in the business they ran together, Stewart refused to go into business with his older brother, but they still had the same battles as the older generation brothers had. In later years, Stewart and his father became drinking buddies and commiserated with each other about the unfairness of life.

Only children, with no siblings to react to, tend to develop more of the characteristics of their same-sex parent than do other children. The only girl child whose mother is an oldest is likely to be more serious and more academic than an only girl whose mother is a youngest and is more playful and flighty.

b. BEING AWARE OF BIRTH ORDER

Until recently, there has been little general discussion of the effects of birth order on personality. However, we have probably always been intuitively aware of them. One of the best places to see evidence of this is in the many biographies and autobiographies that unintentionally provide almost clinically accurate descriptions of people according to their birth order.

One of the most striking examples of this can be seen in the writing of historian Ariel Durant. Her descriptions of her siblings in her autobiography, *Will and Ariel Durant: A Dual Autobiography* reveal their birth order characteristics very clearly. She wrote that her oldest brother, 13-year-old Maurice, was a "good" and "hard-working" boy who had his own newsstand. He "bore the labor of the day without a word of complaint...."

The next oldest, a sister, "became head of the family and served as little mother, watching over us with a fear-full [sic] love," while the parents and Maurice were at work.

Sarah, who was two years older than Ariel, "seemed eons apart." Ariel commented that she never realized until Sarah nursed her how loyal and affectionate Sarah could be.

Ariel described herself as "open, brash, loud, simple, and talkative." Following Ariel was the "frisky" Mary, "blessed with a pretty face." Michael, the youngest, was "cheerful through whatever trials," and as an adult the "joy" of Ariel's old age.

Once you begin to think and talk about birth order characteristics, you realize that you may already be more aware of them than you thought.

4
OLDER AND WISER: OLDEST CHILDREN IN GENERAL

Some people do not make good children. They should spring upon the world fully grown, preferably with a gin and tonic in hand, and conversation in full swing....

Margaret Morley, *Larger than Life —*
A Biography of Robert Morley

People in the birth order of oldest children are probably among the most over-studied sibling groups in the world. Researchers have shown great interest in oldest children for many years, and there is general agreement among them about the characteristics that are common to most oldest children. However, the majority of the studies have used oldest males as subjects, and they haven't taken into account the differences in sex of the oldest or of the following siblings. They have generalized from male oldests to all oldests.

But the sex of the oldest and the sex and number of siblings who follow the oldest play a crucial role in the final personality development, as the following two chapters on oldest brothers and oldest sisters illustrate.

a. GENERAL CHARACTERISTICS

From ancient times, the oldest child has had a special significance in the family — and in the world. This special significance has meant everything from inheriting the kingdom to being offered as a sacrifice in religious rites, which is a good metaphor for the mixed blessings of the oldest.

The oldest child — the first child — is like a first love. The relationship between the first child and parents can never be duplicated. It is replete with the awe and wonder of having brought into the world this little being, the focus of the parents' dreams and hopes. Even if later children become more favored by the parents, the relationship is usually not as intense as with the first child.

For the first few years, oldest children receive the full, undiluted force of their parents' love, fears, and expectations. The parents are usually very excited about the birth of the first child (unless it came too early in the marriage or was the cause of a "shot-gun wedding") and look forward to it with eager anticipation mingled with fear.

Even before the birth, the first pregnancy elicits more excitement and more anxiety than later pregnancies. Prospective first parents usually worry at a minimum about the health of the mother and fetus, what to expect during delivery, whether the baby will be whole and normal at birth. And these concerns are not unfounded. The first is usually the most difficult labor, averaging 14 hours compared to 8 hours for later births, and there are more difficulties with delivery and more abnormalities in newborn firsts.

After the birth, the new parents worry about what kind of parents they will be and whether their child will develop normally.

The parents pay close attention to everything that happens with the first baby — the first smile, the first word, the first step are all exclaimed over, celebrated, and recorded in the baby book. Everything is special and wondrous. This feeling about the oldest child's accomplishments can go on for life, through first graduations, marriage, birth of grandchildren, and so on. Later-born children are taken for granted more, and each successive child usually receives less attention and praise for these routine accomplishments.

Parents are more likely to see their first child as a reflection of themselves so they push the oldest to excel. Oldests usually do walk and talk earlier and are toilet trained sooner than later children in the family.

An oldest boy often has the additional burden of being his father's alter ego even to the point of being given the same name and being expected to follow in father's footsteps whether his feet fit them or not.

But the first child is also the grand experiment. The parents don't really know what they're doing. As one playwright said, "Children ought to be like waffles; you throw away the first one." The parents want desperately to do well with the first one, but their lack of experience makes them more anxious and tense about their parenting, and this is communicated to the child. The parents are often overprotective and too indulgent with their first, while at the same time they have high expectations and often punish the child for not living up to their demands.

Even if the effects are mixed, oldest children have the benefit of the exclusive attention of their parents for several years. Then, just when they have become accustomed to their privileged position with their parents, they are displaced by a new baby. When this displacement comes between the age of 18 months and 4 or 5 years, it is an extreme shock to the oldest child. After 5 years, the oldest has a place in the world outside the family and a well-established identity, so is less threatened by the newcomer.

For the first child who is under 5 years old, the birth of a second child changes everything. Parents suddenly become less available and apparently less interested in the oldest child. Their attention and energy focus on the new little thing in the crib. The behavior of the oldest starts being judged more harshly, and the parents' love seems to become more conditional.

The oldest who does fairly well with this transition has usually found a way to connect better with dad at this point. This is, of course, dependent on dad being physically and emotionally available. If, in the process of "losing" mom to the newborn, the oldest can get more time and attention from dad, then the arrival of a new sibling is not a total loss. If this happens when the oldest is becoming aware of and more oriented to the world outside the home (usually dad's domain in our society), the shift can fit nicely with the child's own developmental needs and interests.

Oldests are often confused following the birth of a sibling. They don't understand what is happening to their world. They feel abandoned at first, then jealous. What they thought was theirs is no longer theirs in the same way. No matter how well the parents have prepared them for the baby, they usually don't see any need for more children in the family, especially helpless, feeble ones who can't even play with them. They wonder why their parents weren't satisfied with them. Why do their parents need another one?

The usual reaction when the baby has been home for a few days is "Send that kid back where he came from." And oldests don't get over these feelings easily, even if the feelings go underground after a while. In their book *Siblings Without Rivalry,* authors Adele Faber and Elaine Mazlish suggest imagining that a husband comes home one day and tells his wife that he's going to be bringing home a new young wife to join their family — someone she can play with and is sure to love. When the younger woman arrives, he spends all his free time helping her get adjusted to her new home and playing with her. He gives her some of his first wife's clothes and jewelry, and asks the first wife to look after her while he's at work. How would this feel to you if you were the wife?

That husband may continually reassure his first wife that he still loves her, and he certainly wouldn't ask her to leave, but most wives in western cultures would still have trouble accepting this situation. Yet parents expect their oldest child to be mature and understanding about it when they bring home a second child. The first child doesn't want to give up any of the parents' love and attention any more than the first wife does, and will do what is necessary to compete with the intruder.

At first the oldest may try to regain attention by reverting to baby-like behavior and demanding a bottle or asking to sleep in a crib. If that doesn't work, the oldest may have temper tantrums or become hostile and aggressive, particularly toward the baby. Stories of the violent actions of oldest children against their next youngest sibling are legion — the stick poked in the eye, the push off the change table, the dropped baby. This, of course, makes the parents angry at the oldest and even more solicitous of the youngest.

...once I discovered my little sister sleeping peacefully in [my favorite] cradle. At this presumption on the part of one to whom as yet no tie of love bound me, I grew angry. I rushed upon the cradle and overturned it, and the baby might have been killed had my mother not caught her as she fell.

Helen Keller, *Story of My Life*

However, in most families this behavior doesn't work either, so the oldest tries another way to get the parents' attention. This leads to one of the common patterns of oldest children: they try very hard to be good (or perfect) so that their parents will continue to love them rather than their "replacement." They become helpful with the baby in order to earn love. They may become like deputy parents. They give up trying to get what they want for themselves and do what the parents want. Their parents naturally appreciate the new cooperativeness of the oldest and reinforce it by telling the oldest that he or she is bigger and smarter than the newborn and therefore superior. Even though the newborn now gets most of the parents' attention, the oldest gets their approval for being whatever they mean by "good" — quiet, tidy, responsible, helpful, nurturing, grown-up.

The parents expect the oldest to set a good example for younger siblings — to be a big girl or boy now — and to help take care of the baby. As a result, oldest children learn early that the way to get rewards is to do what their parents want — to be helpful and "grown-up." They may begin to identify with the parents as a way of distinguishing themselves from the baby nuisance. This can include taking care of the parents. Oldest child George W. Bush, Jr.'s younger sister died when he was seven, and he was overheard saying to friends that he couldn't come out to play because he had to play with his (grieving) mother.

The pattern may be accentuated as the oldest takes care of successive children in a continuing attempt to win the parents' approval. This can result in an oldest child who resents the burden and feels as an adult that his or her life was sacrificed for the younger children. In any case, the oldest rarely has a chance to be a child very long before becoming a "parent," unless the younger siblings are born many years after the oldest.

When the second child is a different sex, the negative reactions of the first child are not usually as dramatic; there is less direct sense of threat to the status of the oldest and less need to compete. If all the younger siblings are of the opposite sex, the characteristics just described will be moderated considerably. For example, an older brother of sisters is often warmer and more caring than an older brother of brothers.

When the second child is the same sex, however, the threat to the first seems much greater. If the younger ones are all of the same sex, especially if there are two or more, the oldest-child characteristics are usually intensified.

If there are more than five years between the oldest and the next child, the oldest — who has been an only child all that time — is more secure, more sure of his or her place in the world, and more likely to feel reasonably benign toward the newcomer. He or she may even enjoy the younger child.

> I can taste even now the fresh delight of learning the boy's open face, his early laughter, prevailing geniality and the immediate presence of a watchful mind, ready to learn every trick we [Reynolds and his parents] could teach and to thank us steadily with stunts of his own.
>
> Reynolds Price,
> writing about his brother seven years younger
> in *Clear Pictures: First Love, First Guides*

Sometimes an oldest child is able to take advantage of the parents' inexperience and become the power in the family, behaving imperiously and stubbornly with the parents and the younger children. This is most likely to happen where the parents are both youngests and uncomfortable with the experience of being in charge.

Occasionally, the oldest child will end up being a leader of the siblings against the parents. However, most oldests side with the parents against the unruly younger children, though they may go through a period of rebellion when they are teenagers.

The oldest in the family is often disciplined more than younger children. One reason for this is the parents' anxiety and higher expectations. Another is that when other children come along, the added burdens make parents more impatient with the oldest and more likely to expect more from that child. Parents often unjustly blame the oldest when there are fights among the siblings because they think the oldest "should know better." More than one youngest has reported "getting off easy" in the family because all the pressure went on the older children and the youngest slipped through without much friction.

Since oldest children spend more years in the exclusive presence of their parents, they spend more time observing and imitating their behavior. They are consequently the children most likely to be similar to their parents. If the parents are nurturing and warm, they will be like that; if the parents are aggressive and harsh, they will be like that. When their parents are old or dead, the oldest sibling is usually the one that takes on the parents' role of organizing holiday get-togethers, or handling family crises, or running the family business.

Oldest children often end up as guardians of the status quo. They begin by defending their own position in the family against later children, go on to preserving the family traditions and morality for their younger siblings, and may end up trying to protect the status quo in the world. Oldest children have fond memories of the past when they were the only. They do not have good feelings about change. In reaction to that situation, they may become so rigid that they are unwilling to accept any change and unable to compromise.

The closer contact with their parents gives oldests better verbal skills and more exposure to abstract thinking than their younger siblings. As a result, oldests usually adapt better to the learning techniques of school. May Stewart studied 7,000 London school children and found that the older children in two-child families were generally better students than the younger children and stayed in school longer. This higher rate of school "success" was true even though overall there was no difference in IQ between the oldest child and youngest child in the families.

Oldests usually have more privileges than the younger siblings, but also are expected to and do assume more and more responsibility as they grow up. An oldest girl usually has the same responsibilities as an oldest boy — sometimes even more — but not the same privileges.

As adults, oldest children usually have many parental qualities; they can be nurturing and protective of others and they are often able to handle responsibility well and assume leadership roles. More than half the presidents of the United States have been oldest male children, and 21 of the first 23 American astronauts were oldest or only children. The world is often ruled by oldests, which reflects both the liabilities and the advantages of that position. World War II, for example, was conducted by oldest sons Churchill, Hitler, Mussolini, and Hirohito along with only children Roosevelt and Stalin.

This sense of responsibility can also be a burden. Oldest children may turn into perfectionists and worriers, who dare not make mistakes or disappoint their parents (or other authority figures). Stutterers are often oldest children who are so fearful of saying something wrong that they can't say it at all. Oldest children tend to have trouble accepting mistakes by others, too. They are the most likely of the children to internalize their parents' expectations about being good. They conform to what is expected of them and tend to think in terms of what they and others "should" do. They may be trying so hard to achieve and be good in school, for instance, that they neglect to make friends. And, since they soon realize that nothing is ever perfect, many oldests tend to be pessimistic about the world in general and their life in particular.

Jimmy Carter, whose father set "seemingly impossible standards of performance" for him, became a lifelong perfectionist who could never openly rebel against his father's harsh discipline, the Navy's hazings, or Congressional disloyalty, according to biographers Bruce Mazlish and Edwin Diamond. His younger sister says that, "no matter how well Jimmy did, Daddy always said he could do better. Daddy always wanted Jimmy to go straight to the top."

Youngest brother Billy, however, openly admits to not having Jimmy's drive or his need to succeed. "It does not bother me to lose a softball game; it drives him crazy....I enjoy life."

Oldests also tend to be compulsive to the degree that they can't walk through a room without straightening the picture frames and can't throw away a tin can without washing it first. A large percentage of people diagnosed as obsessive-compulsives are oldest children.

The emphasis on high achievement tends to make oldest children more tense, more serious, more reserved, and less playful than others. They usually work hard and are conscientious at whatever they do. They have learned to associate fun and play with the immaturity of their youngest siblings. Super-achiever Meryl Streep has been called one of the most intelligent and perceptive actresses in Hollywood. The oldest sister of two brothers, she "looked like a mini-adult" as a child and had a "bossy streak." One of her brothers referred to her as "pretty ghastly."

If the standard of achievement in a particular family is measured by success in crime, the oldest will be a high achiever in that. The oldest may become the "godfather" or a gang leader.

The important thing for oldests is to have the admiration and respect of others. If it doesn't come naturally, they may seek a position of authority in order to demand respect. They often appear to be arrogant when they are actually seeking reassurance.

Because failure seems so devastating to oldests, they find it difficult to accept even constructive criticism or to admit it when they are wrong. Oldests are often overfunctioners, which means that they take on responsibility for other people's lives and problems as well as their own. They try to solve other people's problems even though they don't have the power to make their own solution work in someone else's life. Other people often see these attempts to help as bossiness or intrusiveness, even when the intentions are good.

Oldests often have trouble turning down requests and over-commit themselves rather than disappoint someone. Some oldests feel they have to do it all and meet the needs of work, family, community, and church. Many an oldest child is the pillar of a community and the cornerstone of a church or other volunteer organization. They can't say no, and they can't understand why others don't have the same dedication that they do. They will take on responsibilities and do work that really belongs to someone else. They often resent how much they have to do and how little time they have for themselves, but they aren't able to stop. If anything goes, it is usually their relationships, which get sacrificed to the higher goal of achievement and success.

This tendency to over-commit may arise from their concern to take care of others. Some oldests are so concerned about being nurturing and pleasing others that they seem to be compliant. They allow themselves to be overworked in the same way they were overparented and are often pushed to their limits. They feel responsible for everything and think that if they don't take care of it, it will fall apart.

Alternatively, they may be seeking recognition through trying to accomplish more than others do. They can be so goal-oriented and driven to succeed that they sacrifice themselves, their family, and their employees in order to be the best, the biggest, the richest, or even the most giving and sacrificial.

They don't easily ask for help. They have trouble trusting in the ability of others, and even if they are able to delegate work, they aren't able to delegate their anxiety about the work being done right. After all, their younger siblings could never do anything as well as they could.

Pierre was the oldest of six brothers and sisters and he was strongly encouraged by his father, also an oldest, to become like him — a demanding, directive, take-charge person. Pierre's mother was often unable to function as a parent due to her serious depression. She was frequently hospitalized and absent from the family for long periods. Pierre was often the person who ran the household during these times. He became caring and helpful as well as a take-charge decision maker who organized his younger siblings to do the household chores. The more pressure he felt due to his mother's absence and his father's demands, the more organized and directive he became.

Later, he married a younger sister of a brother, who at first enjoyed Pierre's leadership qualities. She felt safe and well taken care of by him as she had with her brother whom she admired. Over the years, however, she began to have bouts of depression and lethargy, during which Pierre ran the household. She started thinking that her identity was being eroded by Pierre's take-charge way of organizing their lives. She did not know much about his childhood and simply began to think he was a born dictator.

During a number of therapy sessions, Pierre began to be aware of the anxiety that lay behind his impulse to take over a situation and start giving orders. His entire self-image was at stake. He feared that if he did not fulfill his prescribed role of leader when things got tough, he would not be accepted and the whole family would fall apart. He found his wife's reactions quite puzzling at first because he genuinely believed he was just being loving.

It helped his wife to hear that Pierre's anxiety about being accepted was what lay behind his behavior. She learned to see his actions in a different light. Although he felt tremendously vulnerable, Pierre eventually learned not to go into automatic take-charge mode when things got rough. He learned to feel more comfortable with his vulnerability and to appreciate his wife's abilities and her input into joint decision making.

Even at play many oldest children work hard and are high achievers. It's not enough to jog, they have to run — and win — a marathon. It's not enough to have a friendly game of tennis, they have to attack the ball and demolish the opponent.

They are more likely than others in their family to experience jealousy and express anger. Unless their parents have been abusive physically, oldests most often express their anger verbally, which is quite effective since they tend to have high verbal skills. If they have experienced intense jealousy over the youngest, these feelings may be transferred to other scapegoats in the future — minorities or "welfare bums" — whom the oldest perceives as "getting away with things" and getting ahead "without doing a day's work," just like a younger sibling.

b. AS A SPOUSE

Many oldest children have unhappy marriages. Spouses often find them impatient and demanding. Oldests who only have same-sex siblings have a particularly difficult time because they have no experience of living intimately with the opposite sex.

Oldests usually do better when married to someone who was a youngest or middle sibling and may do quite well if they both had opposite sex siblings. They tend to believe in the importance of marriage and want to stay married no matter what. If the marriage ends, they are prone to strong feelings of failure and guilt.

When married to a typical youngest, oldests often see their spouse as less competent and take over doing everything, but then come to resent having to do everything. Oldests often don't feel loved by their spouses and in their anxiety compensate by dominating the household and trying to be more in charge. They do more of what they are good at, thinking this will bring the love they want.

c. AS A PARENT

Oldests usually want to have children and are responsible parents. They may be very nurturing and loving or overprotective and strict, sometimes harsh, in their childrearing. They often appear to their children as cold and distant people, whereas inside they crave the respect of their children.

They are more likely than others to demand adult behavior in their children. Since they try hard to be a perfect parent, they often pressure children to walk, talk, read, etc., before they're ready.

The oldest children of small families are usually happier parenting than the oldests of large families who may have been overburdened and burned out in childhood by caring for many younger siblings.

d. AS A FRIEND

Partly because they use their power to get their own way and partly because they tend to be undemonstrative and serious, oldest children find it difficult to make friends. They usually have just one close friend. They tend to be sensitive to personal slights. Though anxious to please those in authority, oldests are often less popular generally than those in other birth orders.

Although they appear to be independent, they need the approval of others and without it have a low self-esteem. Researcher Margarete Lautis found in her work with oldests that they were "adult-orientated...serious, sensitive...conscientious." They may be "shy, even fearful or self-reliant, independent and undemonstrative." Their difficulty with revealing their weaknesses inhibits the development of close, intimate friendships. They tend to "keep up appearances" even with close friends because they don't want to lose the admiration of anyone.

Oldests have had the experience of always being the leader of the other children in the family and are used to being the best at everything and having the most power with siblings. Therefore, they are used to being able to say, even demand, what they want and will more often be confrontational than manipulative. Just as they ended up being loyal to their parents, they will be loyal to other people in their life and expect loyalty from others. Often, the merely independent actions of others seem like a betrayal to oldest children who may have been surprised and hurt by the rebellion of their younger siblings.

e. AT WORK

Oldest children tend to choose careers that either put them in positions of authority or allow them to work independently. Their need to perform well makes them so anxious as employees that they tend to do less well than if they are in charge or are working without supervision. As employees they can often find themselves in conflict or at odds with their boss if the boss is not also a hard-working oldest. They know better than their boss about how a job "ought" to be done.

They go into helping professions or leadership positions to gain admiration and respect. They often become managers, ministers, teachers, lawyers, and judges. They also do well in intellectual work that requires disciplined, abstract thought with little emphasis on personal relationships — areas such as engineering, physics, higher mathematics, architecture, and chemistry. They are less often in creative work and if they are, they tend to be more conventional than later-birth-order artists.

Eminent scientists and mathematicians are overrepresented by oldest sons. Well-known theoretical physicist Stephen Hawking, author of *A Complete History of Time,* is the oldest of four children. He grew up wanting to figure out how things worked and developed the modest goal in life of having "complete understanding of the universe."

Oldests are also frequently found in academic careers, especially in medicine, law, and psychology. Pioneering heart surgeon William DeVries is an oldest child. Albert Schweitzer, missionary-physician, philosopher, theologian, and music scholar, was an oldest who combined both the intellectual and the nurturing capacities of oldests in his life's work.

Oldests may seek positions of authority where they can use their natural aura of authority in either an ambitious climb to the top or an idealistic effort to change the world for the better. Oldest child Rene Levesque, former leader of the Parti Quebecois in Canada, fought for the sovereignty of Quebec by leading the separatist movement away from terrorism and into mainstream politics.

f. TO THE PARENTS OF AN OLDEST CHILD

You can help your oldest child most by putting less pressure on him or her to succeed and openly giving more love and approval just for existing. Admit your own mistakes to your oldest to show that mistakes happen and no one is perfect. Avoid criticizing the accomplishments of your oldest or re-doing something he or she has done less than perfectly. Point out what's right about the attempt, not what's wrong. If your oldest bakes a cake, mention how good it tastes, not that it's flat as a pancake. Praise the B on the report card rather than asking why it's not an A. Your oldest is probably already too aware and concerned about not being the best.

Allow your oldest to decide how much he or she wants to help with the younger children; don't force the oldest to babysit. Don't expect your oldest to grow up too quickly; let the child be a child and childishly playful. If you don't like something about your oldest child's behavior, check your own; there may be a similar pattern.

After siblings have arrived, continue to spend time alone with your oldest child to help him or her feel important as an individual rather than just as a helper.

Oldest children, even as adults, respond well to pleasant surprises. Because they usually plan ahead and work so hard at preparing things, they often can't enjoy themselves when, say, they are finally on vacation. But a surprise excursion planned by someone else for them can make them feel cared for.

g. TO THE ADULT OLDEST CHILD

In general, you would do well to find ways to relax more, lower your standards for yourself and others, and get more fun out of life. The song "Don't Worry, Be Happy" was written for you. You need to allow yourself to be happy. You can also try expressing your need for love more directly rather than taking care of others to win their love. That is a roundabout way of doing it, and others may not understand that you have needs too. The oldest sister in the movie *Hannah and Her Sisters* did everything for everybody until she learned that she wasn't really earning their love that way. She found out that her husband didn't think she needed him at all. By doing less, she saved her marriage and her relationships with friends and family.

Your parents are no longer watching your every move and are not the all-powerful discipliners they may have been. If you make a mistake, it won't be the end of the world. Some of the people around you may even appreciate that evidence of your humanity. You are good enough as you are.

Be realistic about what you can accomplish in the time available. Be willing to ask for the help and support of others when you need it. And remember that no one has ever looked back over their lives to say, "I wish I had spent more time at the office" or "more time cleaning house."

5
OLDEST SISTERS

Never praise a sister to a sister, in the hope of your compliments reaching the proper ears.

Rudyard Kipling, *False Dawn*

a. OLDEST SISTER OF SISTERS

1. General characteristics

The oldest sister of sisters often has a hard time of it. First-born girls don't have quite the aura of pride and favor surrounding them that first-born boys have, yet may have just as many expectations for success placed on them.

The oldest sister of sisters is displaced by another female, so the competition with her younger sister may be intense, especially if there is less than four years between them. She is likely to think that the younger sister is getting more attention, more praise, and more privileges than she did, and she may be much more jealous than is warranted.

For a long time I regarded my little sister as an intruder. I knew that I had ceased to be my mother's only darling, and the thought filled me with jealousy. She sat in my mother's lap constantly where I used to sit, and seemed to take up all her care and time.

Helen Keller, *Story of My Life*

The oldest sister may be so worried about the threat to her position that she tries to cover all the bases in being the good child so her parents will continue to love her. One way she does this is by being mother's "little helper." She is also likely to be the one to become "teacher's little helper" when she gets to school. In taking the role of parent or teacher with her younger sister, she often models her behavior after her mother's behavior with her and gets great satisfaction from being the guide and mentor.

She [younger sister] alone endowed me with authority; adults sometimes gave in to me: she obeyed me. I loved studying so much that I found teaching enthralling....Teaching my sister to read, write, and count gave me, from the age of six onwards, a sense of pride in my own efficiency.

Simone de Beauvoir,
Memoirs of a Dutiful Daughter

The oldest sister may continue to treat her younger sister as a child long after they are both old women.

However, having a same-sex sibling can be a benefit to the oldest sister. Competing with another female gives her a better chance of succeeding than if she were competing with a boy. The oldest sister of sisters who comes from a loving home will probably be a bright, strong, and independent woman. She is able to take care of herself and of others.

Since parents often want a boy first, they may be disappointed that she is a girl and expect her to fill the role of oldest boy. She may have become her father's companion, which does not change when the following sibling is also a girl. In fact, as she gets older and is able to do more things with her father, she is likely to feel more secure in her position and less threatened by the younger sister.

If, however, she loses her relationship with her father because he enjoys the younger sister more and favors her or she has to share him with many younger sisters, she is more likely to be hostile toward her sisters. If she is treated harshly by her father, she may treat her younger sisters in the same way.

She often runs interference for her younger sisters and fights the battles over makeup, curfews, and boyfriends with her parents, making these less emotional and difficult issues for her sisters. She may then resent the relative freedom they are given.

If her younger sister is a particularly cute child indulged by both parents, the oldest sister may become aggressive and domineering.

[Elder sister] Molly was not only thought to be more intelligent than her sister, she was also more domineering and more temperamental.

Frances Spalding,
Stevie Smith: A Critical Biography

Although the oldest sister of sisters tries to be helpful, she finds it difficult to accept advice or help from others. She tends to be so well-organized and efficient herself that she thinks others can have little to offer her. Her concern for being good enough leads her to be a hardworking perfectionist. She usually has high standards and takes care of all the little details.

Her pride also may keep her from seeking help from others, such as a counselor, and she will rarely admit to any weakness, even a physical illness. She doesn't usually rebel against the circumstances of her life. If her burdens overwhelm her, she is more likely to turn her stress inward and have physical problems, such as migraine headaches or problems with alcohol.

She is often outgoing and self-confident, or acts that way, and has an opinion about everything — the right opinion. Other people may think of her as "tough," though she would not describe herself that way. Since she always tried to please her parents by being good, she usually continues to be exceptionally tidy as a housekeeper and a dresser. She is the most likely woman to try to be Superwoman and do it all — have the perfect house, perfect marriage, perfect child, perfect job — and succeed. Jacqueline Kennedy Onassis was, for many years, the American ideal of the perfect woman. Four years older than her sister, she was the serious child, the good student, and the poised hostess in the company of adults. Her sister was the vivacious, mischievous one, who married first, but couldn't quite keep up with Jackie who married the future president.

Queen Elizabeth II exemplifies the oldest sister's virtues of devotion to duty, self-sacrifice, and hard work. As a child she was a fairly typical oldest sister of a sister, having had a relatively normal childhood for royalty. She was 10 years old before they knew she was in direct line for the throne following her Uncle Edward's abdication.

She also had the oldest sister's handicaps of shyness and severity. She was so conscientious as a child that she would get out of bed at night to make sure her clothes were in order and shoes lined up straight. When ill, she resisted going to bed because she didn't want to "take the easy way out." As a young child, she kept detailed accounts of her spending money.

She was four-and-a-half years old when her sister Margaret Rose was born. Her parents had hoped the second child would be a boy, so Margaret was little threat to her, and she enjoyed looking after her. In fact, Elizabeth called her baby sister "Bud" because "she isn't a real rose yet, just a bud."

Biographer Robert Lacey says Elizabeth "might have been overshadowed in the public eye if her mother had given birth to a new little prince." As it was, her stature merely increased.

As a child, Elizabeth made sure her younger sister behaved in public by admonishing her to sit still and keep her skirt pulled down. At one garden party, Elizabeth warned Margaret not to laugh if she saw someone wearing a funny hat. Despite Elizabeth's guidance, the young Margaret was irrepressibly vivacious, extroverted, "cheeky," and spoiled by the family.

The pattern continued as adults when Margaret wanted to marry the unsuitable, divorced Peter Townsend and later when she divorced Anthony Armstrong-Jones.

2. As a spouse

The oldest sister of sisters isn't overly interested in men, other than her father, and will tend to be bossy with them. Passive men or men who have suffered loss will be likely to accept her bossiness. They may even bring out the tenderness in her. However, the more sisters she has, the less likely she is to marry or to marry successfully.

She usually has the most comfortable marriage with the youngest brother of sisters. He is used to having women be in charge of decision making, and she can take care of him and run his life without too many objections from him. Queen Elizabeth's marriage to Prince Philip, the youngest brother of four sisters much older than him, seems to have been a wise choice. His wit and dynamic personality have been a good balance for her seriousness.

A youngest brother of brothers will also do. He accepts her leadership and her more "masculine" traits (as our culture defines it), and he may have more ambition than the youngest brother of sisters, which she appreciates. If the youngest brother is too dependent and submissive, the oldest sister may lose respect for him and treat him with contempt.

A male only child is often a good match since he is not used to having peers and will accept her in a mother-like role, and she may helpfully push him to succeed. The oldest brother of sisters is usually too much of a lady's man for her taste.

The most difficult match for an oldest sister of sisters is with the oldest brother of brothers, although they are often attracted to each other. They may appreciate and admire each other's drive and competence, but both usually want to be the driver.

Since neither the oldest brother of brothers nor the oldest sister of sisters is used to intimate peer relationships with the opposite sex, they may find it hard to be very understanding of male/female differences and may dismiss each other with comments like, "All men (or women) are such and such."

These two oldests may both be perfectionists but about different things or about doing the same thing different ways. The oldest-child husband may be fanatical about every blade of grass being in place and every weed pulled in the garden, but leave his dirty clothes all over the bedroom floor as he did in mother's house. His oldest-child wife may not be able to tolerate the messy bedroom, but will neglect to change the oil in her car when necessary because father did those things.

Because they both want to be in charge, they may have constant power struggles, which may take the form of loud fighting or silent resentfulness. Their children will learn a lot about fighting for supremacy.

On the other hand, oldests from healthier families can create a very powerful, achievement-oriented nuclear family. Both parents will have many talents and know how to accomplish things. Their children will catch this drive and ability and profit from their gifts.

Even though she may scare off men, the oldest sister of sisters is usually devoted to her father and his loss is often the worst thing that can happen to her, even worse than the loss of her husband.

3.   As a parent

When the oldest sister of sisters has children, she will probably lose interest in her spouse and turn most of her attention to mothering. She is likely to be an overpowering and overprotective mother, although she can also be nurturing and affectionate. She usually prefers to have girls rather than boys and will get along best with an all-girl family. She may have the most trouble with her youngest child, who doesn't appear to take things seriously enough and, if a girl, may remind her of her own younger sister.

Maureen was the oldest of four girls. She got along fairly well with all but the sister who immediately followed her. They fought constantly from early adolescence on, sometimes quite viciously. Maureen married and had three daughters of her own. When her second daughter, Tricia, reached age 13, Maureen found herself tangling ferociously with her. These battles usually started after an argument between Tricia and her older sister.

Maureen's husband was a middle child with both male and female siblings, and overtly was the peacemaker between Maureen and Tricia. However, he covertly felt sorry for Tricia and admired her when she stood up to her mother, which he could rarely do.

In therapy with the family, agreement was reached that he would stay out of the fights completely. This became especially significant later when Maureen was able to recall that her younger sister and her father seemed to be accomplices, which upset her. It was partly in reaction to that coalition that Maureen tried to cause trouble for her sister. When Maureen was asked what she found upsetting about her daughter's behavior, she instantly responded that Tricia was provocative and nasty just like Maureen's younger sister.

By examining the origins of some of the fights between the oldest sister and Tricia, Maureen was able to see that, even though the oldest sister was often at fault, Maureen always sided against Tricia. Maureen was encouraged to spend some time with her younger sister to find out what life as a child had been like for her — what her pains were. As a result, over a period of time, both mother and daughter developed better relationships with their sisters.

4.   As a friend

Her closest female friends are likely to be youngest or middle sisters of sisters — just like home. A female only child may also be able to accept her authority well enough for them to be friends. She is often able to play a mentoring role with these women. The oldest sister of sisters may have much in common with another oldest sister of sisters, and they can get along well enough if they aren't involved in any projects together where there is likely to be a power struggle over who is in charge.

Constance, the oldest sister of a sister, had known and liked Kiko for a long time. They shared many of the same values and had fun together, but they had so many conflicts (more than Constance had ever had with other friends) that Constance became unhappy about the friendship. Constance was in charge of 15 women in a typing pool, and she also had tremendous conflicts with one of the typists there.

Then Constance found out that both her friend, Kiko, and the typist were also oldest sisters of sisters. She realized that their arguments were usually over the proper way to do things. Constance gave up her friendship with Kiko because she didn't have the energy to deal with it, but she had to deal with the office situation. She finally put the typist in charge of a subgroup in the pool and started asking her advice about work. Things went more smoothly from then on.

The oldest sister's sisters, her children, and her loyal friends are very important people in her life as long as they don't try to rebel against her. She wants to look after them and give them advice — and they had better take it!

If she has played a strongly parental role with her younger sisters, they may rebel against her in later life as though she were a parent. The oldest sister is often surprised by this reaction and doesn't understand why she is being cut off. She may feel hurt and miss the family interaction, particularly if she sees her younger sisters turning to their mother for support instead.

On the other hand, she may feel so burdened by her younger sisters that she pulls away from them. In therapy, Bonnie complained that her older sister, Muriel, wouldn't talk to her and didn't want to see her any more. After a slow patient process of making contact with Muriel, Bonnie learned that Muriel had pulled away out of desperation; she didn't know how to hear Bonnie talk about her problems without feeling the need to help her find solutions. Muriel recognized this as overfunctioning for her sister, but just didn't know how to stop it. In therapy, they learned how to be friends and how to avoid confusion over who was responsible for what.

Oldest sisters are often the ones who keep the family together as adults, especially when the parents are elderly or dead. If the younger sisters don't respond to her attempts to have family holidays and visits, the oldest can feel betrayed.

If the childhood animosity has been too great, the issues that arise when a family member dies, especially one of their parents, can be the final blow to their relationship and end all contact between the sisters.

Sisters whose relationships had less conflict often become closer as they get older and go through family crises and milestones together. It is not unusual for sisters to turn to each other for comfort after they have lost their husbands and even move in with each other. They often find this a more natural, comfortable living arrangement than all their years of marriage were, even if they continue to have the same conflicts they did as children. Margaret Mead's rivalry with her younger sisters decreased as they aged, and they became "chosen and most happy companions."

5. At work

At work the oldest sister of sisters is extremely responsible and competent. She is dependable and will get the job done. She works best for a superior who is an older male; other females will have to accede to her authority. She can be hostile if they don't.

Oldest sisters of sisters often end up in a position of authority over other women — as an officer in the Wacs, a director of nursing, a mother superior, a principal, or any kind of manager or top gun. They are better than most women in the wheeling-dealing business world, and can be ruthless if necessary when at the top. They also are more likely than other females to be politicians, doctors, and counselors.

Some oldest sisters of sisters open up entirely new territory for women. Amelia Earhart, for instance, was the first woman to fly solo on a number of long-distance journeys.

6. To the parents of an oldest sister of sisters

Recognize the special threat that an oldest sister of sisters may feel at the birth of another girl. Help her to be less driven to achieve in order to win approval, and be careful of overloading her with household responsibilities. Sisters often fight over their father's attention, so dad should be conscientious about spending time alone with each daughter and being equally affirming of all of them.

Don't be fooled by her apparent lack of vulnerability, and don't give her the line about how she needs to "be strong for the others" if her vulnerability begins to show.

7. To the adult oldest sister of sisters

Try to let go of some of your responsibilities and trust others to do what's necessary for themselves. Recognize what you are and are not responsible for. Learn to resist the temptation to think you are responsible for it all. Become comfortable with the fact that others do not need to do it as well as you can. Make time for yourself and allow yourself to play more.

Accept your younger sisters as adults and equals and give up your role as leader or parent to them. Let them teach you how to play and be spontaneous if this is difficult for you. Set more realistic goals for yourself and realize that if people criticize you, it is not a catastrophe; it may be more their problem than yours. It's okay to stop trying to be perfect yourself (since you'll never get there anyway), and it's impossible for you to make others perfect — they'll never cooperate, so you might as well give up trying.

b. OLDEST SISTER OF BROTHERS

1. General characteristics

The oldest sister of brothers is usually a strong, independent woman. She is down to earth and sensible, with a healthy ego, though she may at times appear self-effacing. She has a sense of responsibility toward others, but doesn't usually feel she must be a Superwoman like an oldest sister of sisters does.

If her family showed great excitement over the subsequent birth of a boy, the oldest sister may try harder to get father's attention and reject her connection with mother and things feminine, particularly if she had been "daddy's girl" before. She may try to win her father's love by being an exhibitionist, overly pleasing and compliant, or obstreperous and argumentative. She may try to show father that she is as good as a boy and become very competitive with her younger brother. She may subsequently feel competitive with and superior to men all her life.

During that period it was unusual for a girl to excel in athletics. Bess did. She had to, growing up with three younger brothers....She was just as good a ball player as her brothers were, and they knew it.

Jhan Robbins, *Bess and Harry Truman: An American Love Story*

Even if no overt preference is shown for the younger boy, the oldest sister still may detect a hidden pride that the parents have in the boy and need to be reassured that her mother still loves her.

Comedian Lucille Ball was "throughout her life...extremely tense, nervous, sensitive and vulnerable, filled with anxiety and fear," according to her biographer Charles Higham. Her brother was born when she was four, shortly after her father's death. That and the later death of her grandmother added to her pessimism and fears. She had a strict, almost puritan, sense of morality, a rare thing for the Hollywood star she was. Although her field was comedy, she took it very seriously and was a perfectionist. She would insist on doing a scene over and over again even though everyone else thought it was good enough the first time. She wouldn't leave any of the details to others, but knew all about the scenery, the props, the lighting — and when something was wrong.

In most cases the oldest sister of brothers identifies with her mother and her mother's nurturing of the baby boy. She may handle her resentment of him by taking him over and making him her baby, which leads to a lifelong pattern of taking care of not only him but of other men as well. Men become the most important thing in the world to her — her most precious possession. The more brothers she has, the more this is likely to be true. She isn't usually very interested in women. She would rather spend time with a man and always wants one in her life. She wants a man to need her; she may gladly set his goals for him, run his household, and take care of his children — and will give up her own work to do it. An oldest sister of a brother who grows up in a fairly cohesive family will be one of the last to see the value of feminist concerns.

If both parents show a great deal of interest in the boy, it can be damaging for the oldest sister, especially in her adult relationships with men. Linelle was the oldest sister of four boys in whom the parents obviously delighted. Her mother was a younger sister of brothers and her father was an oldest of all boys. They were completely wrapped up in the boys and paid little attention to Linelle. Her first brother was just 14 months younger, giving her scant authority as the oldest. Then, in sixth grade, she was held back a year and repeated it with her brother. From then on, he became the leader and, she says, she "just sort of disappeared in the family." She felt like she didn't really count for them anymore. She tried to get attention by being a second mother and supporting the boys in their endeavors, but all of this was just taken for granted and not seen as being special. In therapy, she had to learn to affirm the clear strengths she did have rather than comparing herself unfavorably to men and thinking only their wishes and needs counted.

2. As a spouse

Men tend to like an oldest sister of brothers because she is a good sport and undemanding; she doesn't usually compete with them but tries to help them get ahead. She is responsible and reasonable, like a mother, and tends to remind men of their mother, so much so that they may not think of her romantically unless she proposes to them. If she had many brothers, it may be hard for her to settle for just one man to marry; she would prefer to have lots of men around. Even if she does marry, she will probably have other men in her life in some way, perhaps acting as a patron for them. She may think they are all children underneath and will be maternal with them, including her adult brothers. It's okay with her if her husband has different interests from her. She usually marries a man who is less social and more work-oriented than she is.

Her feminist friends may try to get her to see how she is "being taken advantage of," but they will have a hard time convincing her; so much of her identity is built around taking care of men, which she may tend to see as a noble or good thing even when done at a cost to herself. Hillary Rodham Clinton's tolerance of Bill Clinton's marital behavior may be related to her position as oldest sister of two brothers.

Her best choice for a husband is the usually the youngest brother of sisters. It's the arrangement they are both used to. She can be the leader, when he wishes, and nurture him, and they are both comfortable with the opposite sex. Problems may arise if she is too domineering or he is too submissive.

Marriage to a youngest brother of brothers usually works also. He is usually willing to let her lead. He sometimes has difficulty with her being a woman, but he usually thinks he has no need to compete with a mere woman. The danger is that the oldest sister of brothers will be too domineering for a youngest son and that he will rebel with some hostility.

Karen, an oldest sister of brothers, was married to an oldest brother of brothers for 15 years. They ran a meat-packing plant together and had two children. While Karen was happy to let her husband be the more prominent person in the public's eye, she had serious clashes with him in private over how to run the plant and their marriage, how to be parents, and how to spend money. After they divorced, Karen married a man who was a boat builder. He was the younger brother of a sister and a brother and was content to let Karen make the major decisions and run the office for him, giving him more time to do the work he loved on the boats.

A middle brother and an only male child are also suitable matches for an oldest sister of brothers. They often like her for her mothering qualities, and she is tolerant of their faults. The male only may withdraw if he finds her too domineering for his independent ways. Eleanor Roosevelt, oldest sister of two brothers, and only child Franklin had many clashes over roles, which eased somewhat when he became paralyzed and she had to take on more responsibilities.

The oldest brother of brothers or of sisters is often a poorer match for her since they may have conflict over who knows best. If she is married to a man in one of these birth-order positions, the arrival of children usually takes away some of the tension.

They both like having younger ones around again and will focus more on the parenting than on each other.

If she loses one of the men in her life, she may grieve deeply, but her life will go on and her easy-going nature usually helps her bounce back relatively quickly. While her father is very important to her, the only death that will really throw her is the death of her mother when she is very young. She needs her mother then as a model for how to satisfy the males in the family.

3. As a parent

The oldest sister of brothers usually wants to have children. They are her second most precious possession after her husband (sometimes even the first if they are boys). She usually enjoys the domestic role and is able to take good care of both husband and children. The children are usually closer to her than to their father.

4. As a friend

Female friends are not often important to the oldest sister of brothers unless they serve some purpose, such as bringing along another man for her to take care of. She may want to help the friend with her man, or, because she knows better how to take care of men, she may win the man away and thus end the friendship. If she does have female friends for their own sake, they are likely to be youngest sisters of sisters, or middle sisters, who can look up to her. She is always eager to solve people's problems for them and is a good listener, knowing how to draw out someone's innermost thoughts and feelings.

Oldest sisters of sisters may try to be friends with her but she's usually not interested unless they have a man she could befriend. A female only child is a good possibility as a friend since she doesn't mind being mothered and will leave the important things (men) to the oldest sister of brothers.

5.   At work

At work the oldest sister of brothers is usually a congenial, though not especially hard, worker. She often goes into careers such as nursing, social work, acting, or personnel. She may act as a mediator when there are conflicts, and she "knows her place" as a female. She is often a good secretary, and may make subtle suggestions for improvement to a male boss while allowing him to take all the credit. She finds teaching a fulfilling job and is usually good at it, as she is at counseling, especially with male clients.

She will help, almost push, smart younger men ahead and is often content to wield her power from behind. If she is in a leadership position, she usually handles it with care, being tactful and delegating work well (often because she doesn't think it worth her time). She tends to be patronizing, especially about "her boys" and will be protective of them. With female workers she is less understanding. She doesn't really worry too much about their happiness.

6.   To the parents of an oldest sister of brothers

When the younger boy is born, be sure to reassure your oldest daughter that she is still loved and respected — and counts. Don't let her think that her younger brother is more important to you by virtue of his sex. You may need to examine your own attitudes toward gender. Do you harbor a secret belief that males are "better" or of greater value than females? Do you prefer your son simply because he is male? Gender bias of this kind has done great damage to women in this birth position over the years. And don't naturally assume that she will be a second mother; encourage her to pursue her own interests and talents.

7.   To the adult oldest sister of brothers

Remember that not all men are your younger brothers. They may neither need nor want you to take care of them. Beware of trying to make decisions for the men in your life or competing with men for the sake of competing. Be more accepting and appreciative of your own sex — yourself and other women. Look for ways to fulfill your life through your own interests and achievement rather than through the men in your life. It's okay for you to be a little selfish. If you build your identity around being a caretaker, you will often augment the underfunctioning of the men in your life and help prevent them from growing up.

Vanessa was an older sister of a brother. Shortly after she married, her husband's elderly mother moved in and lived with them for the next 20 years until she died. To please her husband, Vanessa dutifully took care of her mother-in-law as well as their three children. Shortly after the mother's death, Vanessa's alcoholic brother came to stay with her, and she took care of him until he died. Then her own widowed father came to live with them until he died. Shortly after retiring, Vanessa's husband had a stroke and she began taking care of him. During all of this, her only son was babied and coddled to the extent of never really being able to live independently and successfully on his own. The tragedy of Vanessa's life was that all her sacrifices did not really solve the problems of all the people she was taking care of. Without her help, they might have been forced into living healthier, more independent lives. And she might have had a happier life herself if she had been less unselfish.

c. OLDEST SISTER OF BROTHERS AND SISTERS

This woman is usually less of a queen bee than the oldest sister of sisters and less in need of an older, father-like man in her life. She is often a better, more ambitious worker than the oldest sister of brothers and less likely to coddle men. Sandra Day O'-Conner, first woman judge on the Supreme Court of the United States, is the oldest of a sister and a brother.

This oldest is still an independent, strong woman but will be more at ease with both men and women than the oldest sister of one-sex siblings. Margaret Mead, the oldest of four surviving children, including a brother two years younger, is a good example of this. As a famous and controversial anthropologist in the 1920s and 1930s, Mead pursued a successful career in a man's world and championed women's rights, yet her love relationships with men were also an integral part of her life and work. Mead said she was "wanted and loved" as a first child. Her younger brother, a fragile child, was no threat to the sturdy Margaret, favored by her father.

6
OLDEST BROTHERS

My little Son, who look'd from thoughtful eyes
And moved and spoke in quiet grown-up wise.

Coventry Kersey Dighton Patmore,
The Unknown Eros

a. OLDEST BROTHER OF BROTHERS

1. General characteristics

The oldest brother of brothers is the boss. He is used to being a leader of men (or little boys), and he wants to continue to be in charge in all aspects of his life, either by virtue of his position or his capabilities. The oldest boy in the family, throughout history and in all cultures, has been singled out for special treatment. Even in the first century B.C., Marc Antony, as the oldest of three boys, was pre-ordained to go into politics in Rome.

Whatever the family hopes and aspirations are, the oldest brother of brothers is the one most likely to have the burden of fulfilling them. Wayne Gretzky's father wanted a hockey star in the family even before Wayne was born. He started teaching

Wayne to play at age two-and-a-half and often told him that being a hockey star was worth the sacrifices. Wayne's younger brother played as well, but it is the oldest son in the family who has played the longest and the best. Pavel Bure is also the oldest brother of a brother. His younger brother is said to be a more easygoing, more westernized man.

The oldest brother of brothers is usually quite meticulous in his person and his possessions. He may be a perfectionist in many ways — from wanting the tidiest of houses to wanting to win every game. He can be both more irritable and more irritating than those in other birth positions.

The oldest brother of brothers is likely to be a man much admired by others and sometimes by family. He may just as readily be feared by his family and others because he can be so adult and in control and intimidating. His younger brothers may be angry at him, but keep their distance because they are afraid of confronting him.

When his baby brother arrives, he turns to his mother for reassurance, but sees that she now has to be shared between three males. If he does not receive the reassurance he needs, he may begin to see all women as remote and unreachable. He tries to retain or win his mother's love by pleasing her in any way he can — by being what she wants, asking for her advice, doing well in school or at whatever she values as important. He thus grows up soon and conforms quickly to adult values, becoming well-behaved, serious, and responsible.

He might have been a hundred years old, rather than eleven, so serious, so responsible he was, planning ahead, nothing forgotten or neglected. I listened, a silent lieutenant, proud and adoring.

Richard Church writing about his older brother in *Over the Bridge*

If these tactics don't work, the older brother of brothers may become quarrelsome and rebellious or develop physical problems to get mother's care and attention. To some extent, his ability to get her continued attention will depend on her birth order.

When there are four or five years' difference in age between brothers, the oldest is less jealous of the younger brother and more likely to be a father figure, though more often in the realm of instructing than in nurturing. The greater the age span the more nurturing and less competitive he is with his younger brothers. He may be competitive only with the next oldest brother and nurturing with the others. He may get along well with people outside the family, especially men, but is usually not on intimate terms with anyone — even his brothers. He rarely turns to his brothers in the more vulnerable position of asking for help, even when life gets really rough for him.

The oldest brother of brothers is usually a leader in some way and usually successful at what he does. He can be condescending to others if he got away with treating a younger brother as a servant. The extreme rivalry that can occur between boys makes the two-boy family the most challenging combination for parents, especially for single mothers.

He is good at planning and can spot the flaws in things, organizations, and people. He is most often an organizer and a synthesizer of what exists rather than a radical innovator. He is very goal-directed and tends to see people as parts of a puzzle rather than as companions. He likes to have nice things around him and is likely to accumulate money and possessions — quality possessions.

He tends to identify most readily with father and will model himself along the same lines, especially if father is an oldest. He may even compete with father, thinking he has to be better than dad at what dad is good at.

Kermit, three years my senior, early on paired with our father as a force for order and goodness...my dark mother and I were linked not only in appearance but in our unspoken conspiracy against the restraints and prohibitions of reality.

Arthur Miller, writing about his older
brother in *Timebends*

He believes in law and order (on his terms) and is not uncomfortable with elitism or even a paternalistic dictatorship, especially when it is "for the good of" others. His rigidity may be driven by a strong conscience. He is often conformist, introverted, and respectful of authority. Oldest son Ludwig von Beethoven was quiet, obedient, and shy as a child, engrossed in his music, but unhappy in his life. He followed in the footsteps of his father and his grandfather, both successful musicians.

If the oldest brother does "misbehave" in any way according to the norms of his family, he is often tortured by guilt. One oldest brother who confessed in therapy to having had an affair almost killed himself in his remorse. "I never would have thought myself capable of such a treachery," he said.

These characteristics seem to cross national boundaries and have shown up in studies of oldest sons in North America, the Netherlands, and Austria.

2. As a spouse

The oldest brother of brothers is often a Humphrey Bogart character with women: indifferent and diffident on the surface, but secretly hoping they will fall for him. He won't usually admit it or ask for it, but he likes women to mother him. He tends to expect a lot from a wife, but usually gives little. In his need to command respect he may belittle his wife. Since he seldom has many intimate friends, he may not know how to be good friends with a wife and will be awkward with her, as he often is with other women. Sometimes his only way of being intimate is to be bossy. Even though he doesn't openly appear to be dependent on his wife, he is often possessive and is the most likely husband to want his wife at his side at all times. Her care, attention, and support are much more important to him than he usually lets on.

The oldest brother of brothers often chooses a woman who is most like a little brother. She may even look slim and boyish. He is usually best matched with the youngest sister of brothers who may be a tomboy, though she is also cute, and, of course, likes men very much. Their rank positions are well matched, and he will consider the difference in sex just something else that makes him the superior. However, for it to work, she must be willing to cater to him more than a youngest sister usually does, and if he ridicules or ignores her ideas and contributions to the family, she may rebel and leave — emotionally if not physically.

Oldest brother of a brother Johann married Brigitta, the youngest of a sister and brother. For ten years, everything was stable in their marriage. Johann worked hard as an architect, putting most of his energy into the business. Brigitta took care of their two children, cleaned house, and entertained Johann's clients. Then, with the children in school, Brigitta started taking courses at a nearby college — and she began to change. She had never been completely happy with her function in the family, which was to run the household smoothly — the way Johann wanted it. She wished that she had more say in the decision making, she didn't like the way Johann treated the children, and she wanted to do less business entertaining and more social things with the people she was meeting at school. As she began to be more self-confident, she started asking for things to be different. But Johann liked the way things had always been and didn't want Brigitta or their lifestyle to change. He refused to discuss it with her. Brigitta finally rebelled completely and left Johann, his big Tudor house, his cabin cruiser, and his closet full of three-piece suits. Johann was furious at first, then he tried everything he was capable of to woo her back. When that failed, he just devoted himself to work.

The oldest sister of brothers is sometimes a good match since she is maternal with men. Their conflicts will probably be over who knows best, though she will try to humor him along. The most difficult match is usually with the oldest sister of sisters; there are rank and sex conflicts for both of them. They often relate to each other like two sovereign monarchs forced to share a castle together. At best, they may respect each other and admire each other's accomplishments, but the more like typical oldests they are, the more likely it is they will have a rather stiff and formal relationship. At worst, it is all-out war. They do best when they each seek approval and admiration in outside interests rather than from each other.

The more younger brothers the oldest brother of brothers has, the more difficult it will be for him to marry or stay married. If he doesn't marry, he is likely to have many younger women around — probably working for him.

3. As a parent

The oldest brother of brothers is comfortable in the role of being a parent and willingly takes on the responsibility, if not actually the daily chores, of caring for children.

He is usually better as a father with boy children or, at least, boys first then girls. Regardless of their sex, he is usually a strict, conservative parent, much more authoritarian than his wife (unless she is the oldest sister of sisters), and the children — especially the oldest who will try so hard to be like him — may often feel misunderstood by him.

The more rigid he is the more likely he is to have major conflicts with his sons and be disappointed in them. If he was able to dominate his brothers, physically and emotionally, he will be quite frustrated that in this day and age his own sons won't take it, and this could lead to a serious rift between them.

Bill Cosby, one of television's most successful and richest stars, has also become famous as a parent through his book *Fatherhood*. As a teenager, he became both father and mother to his two younger brothers when his father deserted the family and his mother had to work 14 hours a day to support them.

4. As a friend

The oldest brother of brothers is seldom the most popular person in a group, but he is likely to have strong, not close, male friendships organized around some typically male activities. His best friends are usually younger brothers of brothers, although he has greater respect for men who share his birth and gender order or for male only children. He may in later life develop a stronger bond with his brother, although the relationship may continue to be a mixture of taking care of, ordering around, teaching, and being exasperated with little brother.

> My [elder] brother was one who looked ahead, and liked things to be in proportion and complete....never satisfied until he had collected all possible information on everything....

> Father picked me up and carried me like a baby. I knew Jack would...accuse me of showing off or creating a scene. He had a horror of any form of demonstration, and he discouraged extravagance and self-indulgence — two weaknesses he was always prepared to detect in me, and to correct.
>
> Richard Church, *Over the Bridge*

He is not likely to turn to others for help, though, or ever seek counseling; he doesn't like being in a dependent position of any kind. Most oldest brothers of brothers who get involved in counseling tend to do it to "help" others (wife or children) straighten out their lives and will rarely think of themselves as having a problem or being part of the difficulty.

5. At work

Although as a young child the oldest brother of brothers is the one most likely to balk at going to school and leaving mother behind with baby brother, he usually deals with the situation by becoming a good student and working hard to advance himself. Paul McCartney worked hard and did well in school despite a disadvantaged background, while his younger brother just got by; Paul then went on to become a superstar with the Beatles.

At work the oldest brother of brothers usually either accepts the authority of a male superior by emulating him and becoming a right-hand man or tries to usurp the superior's position and take over himself. If he sees opportunities for promotion, he works hard as an employee and competes with his co-workers for the admiration of a supervisor, just as he did for his parents' approval.

This oldest may have conflicts with people in authority over him and works best as an independent without a boss. He is likely to end up as a lawyer, a minister, an economist, a politician, or as the president of a company or country. He is most likely to excel in the sciences. He wants his work to be recognized and live on after he is dead. As a result, he often overextends himself at work, and he is just as often very successful.

As a boss he demands much from his workers, is upset by mistakes or excuses for poor work, and expects loyalty, which he rewards well. His hard-driven approach to work and business sense may bring him success, but he can have difficulties and possibly make life harder for himself because of his inability to relate well to others.

6. To the parents of an oldest brother of brothers

Make sure you allow your oldest son to make mistakes and praise him in spite of them. Encourage him to play for the sake of play and give him enough of your attention and approval so that he doesn't have to be bossy or overachieving to get it.

Don't put him in charge of his brothers too often or hold him up as a model for them. He will be very sensitive to any belief you have that he is to be the family standard bearer and carry on its traditions for your sake. Let him be a little boy — when he is — and encourage him to talk about his fears and worries. Listen sympathetically to his problems so that he can have the experience of connecting with others when he feels vulnerable.

He will tend to learn about how men relate to women by watching how his father relates to his mother. Fathers, you need to be clear about what kind of lessons he is learning from your behavior with women.

7. To the adult oldest brother of brothers

You don't have to keep being the best at everything and saving the world. You no longer need to win your parents' approval. Accept yourself as you are and relax. Think about what difference your perfectionism will make to anybody 100 years from now. Your burdens will be lighter if you accept your mistakes, admit them, and apologize when you are wrong — and let others do the same.

If you want to stop being alone emotionally and get closer to others, you need to learn how to be more comfortable with and open about your own vulnerability. You may be incorrectly assuming that others know how tough life can be for you; but they don't know if you don't tell them.

Try not planning, not anticipating, but just letting things happen spontaneously. Let yourself go a little — do things just for the sake of having fun, not to win or meet a personal goal. Be self-indulgent and practice spending money "frivolously." Since women are a relative unknown to you, be open to letting them teach you what they know of life.

b. OLDEST BROTHER OF SISTERS

1. General characteristics

The two-child family of older boy, younger girl seems to be the least difficult combination for parents. The oldest brother of sisters tends to become a much more easygoing and fun-loving man than the oldest brother of brothers, and the older

He is generally open about himself with others and willing to accept help from friends. He is one of the most likely men to seek therapy and usually does well with a woman therapist.

5. At work

This man is usually a good worker, especially if there are women around, but he doesn't usually work overly hard. He likes to be the leader, but is an easygoing superior who wants the work done, yet not at the expense of enjoying it.

He can work well for a female superior if she is somewhat submissive to him and openly admires him. He also works well for a male who is much older, like a father, or for a man who is clearly the superior worker.

He is often happiest in jobs where there are a lot of women around, such as in the theater, the ballet, or the church. He may also be good in public relations and advertising, but his best work perhaps is as a pediatrician or an obstetrician/gynecologist.

6. To the parents of an oldest brother of sisters

Make sure that you do not exhibit preference for the older son because of his sex and spoil him; give him the appropriate amount of household responsibilities so he doesn't expect to be waited on by his younger sister and other women all his life. Encourage him to spend time with other boys as a child and make sure he spends plenty of time in activities alone with his father.

7. To the adult oldest brother of sisters

Don't expect all women to be like your sister — for good or ill. Learn to see what you may think of as "weakness" from a less superior stance. Be willing to share authority and decision making with your wife and accept that she may not always feel the need of your benevolent protection. Realize that she can probably run her own life without your help, even though she enjoys your company.

c. OLDEST BROTHER OF BROTHERS AND SISTERS

This man is usually comfortable with both sexes, especially those who are younger siblings of older brothers. Depending on the number of younger siblings and the sex of those closest to him, he can be a strong leader of men or a more nurturing, encouraging mentor of both men and women. He willingly takes on responsibility, frequently too much too soon, and sometimes seems to be or wants to be father to the world.

> But her eldest son had never learned to weep....Amazingly, for a boy of nine and a half, he told himself: "If I don't help my family, who will?" Within weeks...David was handing over to his mother little fistfuls of pennies each night....
>
> He put away childish things when he was barely five and had plunged into the worries of maturity...when he was barely ten. He never had the leisure to learn to play, to swim, to join friends in outings or exuberant mischief.
>
> Eugene Lyons, writing about David Sarnoff, oldest of four boys and a girl, in *David Sarnoff: A Biography*

Dr. Benjamin Spock, the pediatrician who taught a generation of mothers how to parent in *The Book of Baby and Child Care*, was the oldest brother of two brothers and four sisters. "Like the first child in any big family, I loved playing parent. I grew up taking it for granted that kids were very important," he said.

The oldest brother of brothers and sisters tends to be a compassionate leader and attract a loyal and devoted following as, for example, Billy Graham, oldest of two sisters and a brother. In the biography, *Billy Graham*, his wife is quoted as saying that even when young, he was, "a mature man ... he was a man who had a purpose, a dedication in life; he knew where he was going."

The oldest brother of brothers and sisters is less taken with women and is less irresistible to them than the oldest brother of only sisters. Prince Charles, followed by a sister, then two brothers much later, seems to be less patient with women than many oldest brothers of sisters. He and sister Anne always had a "combustible" relationship, even though at age five he was told to look after her, and did act protectively toward her. However, her stubbornness, petulance, and public outbursts disturbed him greatly. He "thought she didn't understand her job and responsibilities," says biographer Anthony Holden. And Prince Charles didn't seem to appreciate the exuberance of a wife who was considerably younger than him and was the youngest of three sisters, with one younger brother.

This oldest brother is usually an easier husband, a more relaxed father, and less of a dogmatic perfectionist than the oldest brother of brothers; he is also a harder worker, a more ambitious career man, and more likely to be one of the guys than the oldest brother of sisters.

Isaac Asimov epitomizes the mixed characteristics of this birth position. An excellent student he was more involved with books than friends. Yet he nursed his younger sister through illnesses and taught her to read so well she started school in second grade; he also cared for his infant brother (pushing him in a carriage while reading *The Iliad*) when his parents were at work in their store.

Because Isaac read so much as a child, his father accused him of being lazy and not helping enough in the store. As an adult, Asimov worked ten hours a day, seven days a week. If he had to stop working for some reason, he got uneasy, "as though I hear a voice within me saying `Who's watching the store?'" he said in his autobiography, *In Memory Yet Green*.

7
OH, YOU BEAUTIFUL BABY: YOUNGEST CHILDREN IN GENERAL

Alas! they were so young, so beautiful,
So...loving, helpless.

George Gordon Byron, Don Juan

a. GENERAL CHARACTERISTICS

Youngest children, like only children, are never displaced by a newborn. They are always the baby of the family. Most of them continue to look young or cute even when they are old. Actress Bernadette Peters was plagued by critics calling her "cute," "adorable," and "a Kewpie doll."

The families of youngests may also continue to baby them long beyond babyhood and introduce them to others as "the baby." Youngest child Dick Clark is known publicly as "America's oldest living teenager."

Because they are the baby, youngest children are special members of the family in a way that oldest and middle children are not. They often get a lot of attention because everyone else in the family feels some responsibility for taking care of the youngest. Just being the youngest means they are the cutest, and they are often pampered longer than they should be. They may be treated like the family pet or mascot. And, in fact, they are the most likely children in their family to want a pet of their own — something they can take care of, perhaps boss around. They also cope the best with the messiness and unpredictability of animals.

Parents are usually more relaxed as parents by the time the youngest is born, even if the youngest is just the second. They don't panic at every sniffle and they don't have as much anxiety about doing everything right. They are also more tolerant of mistakes and put less pressure on this child to walk, talk, and be toilet trained early. Their pride is still the oldest, but their joy is the charming youngest. In surveys, parents usually describe their youngest as an easier child to raise and more fun to be with.

When Isaac Asimov was young his father wouldn't let him read "trash" like science fiction. By the time the youngest boy was born, Asimov writes in his autobiography, "...my father had lost some of the verve of youth, and having expended himself on the battle with me, let him read whatever he wanted. He read comics...."

Youngest children are often indulged more than the other children in the family were, but they are not usually spoiled in a negative way. They just learn to expect good things from life, so usually end up being great optimists as well as hedonists. Youngests often expect, and get, help from other people even without asking. They just look helpless and people rush to their aid. They don't need to make much effort on their own.

Leandra, a youngest who doubted her intellectual capacity, didn't bother to study issues or form opinions herself, but asked others what they thought about things and then repeated their positions as her own. People, especially men, were flattered to be asked their opinions and happily obliged her, so she rarely had the challenge of thinking through things on her own.

Youngest children usually receive the least discipline of the siblings and less physical punishment, especially if there were many older children. In contrast to the older children, they are more often disciplined by mother than father, and mother has usually relaxed some of the rules by this time. This is often a cause of dissension between siblings. The older ones sometimes resent the apparent laxness and feel that the youngest "can get away with anything."

As a result of this more relaxed attitude, "rules" have less meaning for youngest children. Even as adults they often think the rules are meant for other people, not for them. They are inclined to break social rules as well and will take playful potshots at the establishment without being directly confrontational. Youngest child David Niven was known for his practical jokes, such as having a prostitute pose as a mother at his prep school's Parents' Day. He was a mischievous schoolboy who was eventually expelled for cheating.

Youngests are also more likely than others to be undisciplined in their personal life, procrastinate continually, and be late for or miss appointments.

However, youngest children often remain dependent on others even if they do rebel against the rules. They often choose older spouses and then fight against their control. A youngest might seek out expert advice but then argue against it. In any lecture about birth order characteristics, the audience members most likely to dispute research findings are the youngests.

The youngest of two is usually resented by the older sibling more than the youngest in a larger family where each new baby induces less jealousy. Some youngests in a larger family see the oldest sibling as a hero and try to please or emulate that child more than the parents.

As the youngest, Paul [Robeson] was the doted-upon favorite, and in later life always spoke of his family with deep affection. The firstborn...became a physician.... Paul later credited him as the most "brilliant" member of the family and his own "principal source of learning how to study."

Martin Bauml Duberman, *Paul Robeson*

If the family has been too solicitous, youngest children may have unrealistic expectations of other people they encounter in later life who do not dote on them or treat them as well as the family did.

If the family teased them too much or too unkindly or ran life for them, youngests may rebel against others and be "out to show them." Some just become shy and uncertain and continue to think of themselves as small and incompetent even when grown. As children they don't understand that eventually they will be able to do everything as easily as the older siblings; they see only their present incompetence and get frustrated by their lack of success. They may lose hope for the future and give up trying. If they are forced to follow in the footsteps of an older sibling or if they are not talented in some way, they feel even more frustrated and inadequate.

The youngests may also be sensitive in later life to the issue of fairness if they think they are being held back while the older children are given privileges and freedoms they want.

If they were always on the receiving end of hand-me-down clothes and toys, having high-quality clothes and flashy toys (e.g., cars) may become overly important to them as adults.

Whether or not that was the case for Dick Clark, he certainly enjoys "the best," with his Rolls Royce, Mercedes-Benz, and Jaguar. His three marriages are another common pattern of youngests.

Youngest child and youngest Beatle George Harrison was a flashy dresser as a teen and the first in his school to have long hair. He liked to stand out and had little respect for authority, often getting into trouble.

Because they grew up as the smallest in the family, youngest children learn early that it doesn't necessarily work to be aggressive to get their way. They develop a manipulative style of getting what they want, either by pouting or by being charming, and sometimes by fibbing or being sneaky. As youngsters, they may try to get on the side of their parents by telling on their older siblings and playing the victim.

If their family was happy, youngest children are the most likely of their siblings to be lighthearted and playful and have high self-esteem. They usually have an adventurous approach to life and are open to trying new things. Underwater explorer and youngest child Jacques Cousteau is a perfect example of this.

b. AS A SPOUSE

When youngest children are married to each other, they may appear irresponsible to others, as they don't take homemaking and childrearing too seriously. They are more interested in having a good time themselves, and often do. They can be having such a good time that they get into debt or lose their jobs, or in some other way violate society's expectations for them to act responsibly. The resulting outside pressures then create friction between them. Princess Margaret and the Earl of Snowdon, both youngest of a sister, were finally driven to divorce partly in spite of, but partly because of, the tremendous pressure on them to stay married.

The oldest child of such a couple may end up being the adult in the family and is often wiser and more responsible than the parents.

Youngests are the most likely to have a parent die while they are still young since their parents are older during their childhood. This was the case with both Pat Nixon and Lady Bird Johnson, each the youngest of two brothers. Youngests may suffer greatly from this early loss and later marry an oldest parent figure to compensate. Such a marriage often doesn't work.

With the curious smile [in a family photo], I mean to conceal my secret career as guide and defender of my two young parents, helpless as babes...I cherished my father and mother more than anything else.

Oldest child Reynolds Price, writing about his parents, both youngests, in *Clear Pictures: First Love, First Guides*

c. AS A PARENT

Youngests are not automatically enthusiastic about having children, but they can be relaxed, enjoyable parents to have. They tend to be less concerned about the child's safety and achievements and have a more laissez-faire attitude to childrearing. Some children may interpret this as their parents' lack of interest in them. However, youngests are usually understanding parents and give their children more freedom than other parents.

My parents took no responsibility for me...I never suffered the meddlesomeness of those morbidly conscientious parents who are so busy with their children's characters that they have no time to look after their own. I cannot remember having ever heard a single word uttered by my mother in the nature of moral or religious instruction.

She did not concern herself much about us, for she had never been taught that mothering is a science, nor that it matters in the least what children eat or drink.

George Bernard Shaw, writing about his parents, who were among the younger siblings in their large families, in *Shaw: An Autobiography 1856-1898*

Youngests as parents often have trouble being consistent with their children. They may compete with them for attention.

A youngest parent may not appreciate the seriousness and domineering nature of the oldest child and take the side of the younger sibling in any disputes. On the other hand, youngests can also be playful with their children and enjoy them.

In Chekhov's play, *The Seagull,* the youngest-sister mother of the protagonist doesn't take the writing efforts of her son seriously and actually sees his play writing as an infringement on her territory as an actress. She is not only unable to affirm his efforts, but she competes with him. His efforts to win her approval are as futile as his efforts to win the love of the woman he wants to marry. His despair ends in suicide.

If the other parent is an oldest, there may be conflicts because that parent will think the children are too sassy, too messy, too careless. An oldest man married to a youngest woman may think she is too lenient with the children. If she is uncertain of her parenting abilities, she may resent the active role he takes as a parent. If the other parent is an only child, a youngest spouse may feel the need for the only-child partner to be more involved with the children.

d. AS A FRIEND

Youngest children who have been treated well as children are usually the most sociable, easygoing, and popular of the birth orders. Since they are used to having at least three other people around since birth, they generally enjoy being in groups. However, if they are from a very large family they may resent the lack of privacy and feel as though they are being hounded or spied on, and want to do things in secret.

If they have been unkindly teased as the youngest, they may be shy and irritable with others. If their parents badly wanted them to be a child of the opposite sex, the youngest of all one sex may have more characteristics of both sexes than most or may just feel generally inadequate and therefore not comfortable with other people.

Sometimes the youngest may have trouble breaking into the family structure. The parents are at the greatest distance from the youngest child and if the older children have already worked out their relationships, the youngest may feel left out and left behind. If there are several older children, the youngest may feel there is no role left to fill. In these cases, the youngest may be shy and introverted or alienated and unable to make friends easily.

e. AT WORK

By the time the youngest child arrives, the parents have had experience in parenting, so they are both less awed by the baby's accomplishments and more relaxed about being parents. They are able to sit back and just enjoy this one or, if they are bored with children by this time, ignore him or her.

We all [in a group home for refugee children] had a little patch of garden which we cultivated ourselves. Mine never seemed to grow anything, and everybody else's looked fantastic. I suppose being the youngest I did everything wrong, nothing grew.

Sarah Moskovitz, *Love Despite Hate,*
Child Survivors of the Holocaust and
Their Adult Lives

Regardless of their reasons, the parents usually have fewer expectations of the youngest throughout childhood and put much less pressure on the youngest to achieve great things. And so, as you might guess, youngests usually do achieve less. They realize early on that no one is impressed by their childhood accomplishments — it's all been done before and nothing they do is significant — so they stop trying to excel and look for affirmation in other ways.

Some youngests also get a subliminal message from the family that they shouldn't be better than the oldest so they don't let themselves succeed.

If not pushed, most youngests just get by as students and may be the class cut-up or delinquent. Since they may feel better about themselves when in the company of other low achievers, they can end up running in a bad crowd.

They are the least career-oriented of the birth orders. They tend to look for work that is not too demanding, something that will fit in around their life of leisure activities. An exception is the youngest in a larger or poorer family. By the time this youngest is ready for higher education or career selection, there may be more money available and all the older siblings may help support the family's last hope for success.

Most youngests, however, know from the beginning that their parents are shared, and they try to get attention by being different from the older siblings. Since older siblings, especially in a two-child family, are high achievers, youngests look for other ways to stand out. They may do this most effectively by being a troublemaker since being smart has already been done. Generally, though, youngests find that they get more attention by being cute or funny. As a result, they are seldom taken seriously and as adults often crave respect. They may become fast, voluble talkers to try to get people to pay attention to what they have to say. They often go into sales work because of their innate knowledge about what hooks people's attention and their ability to out-talk others.

In some ways, youngests try unsuccessfully to catch up with their elder siblings for the rest of their lives. When 30-year-old Janie went bike riding with some friends, the rest of the group wanted to go all the way to the reservoir dam at the end of the road. But Janie, who hadn't done much riding recently, was tired and told them to go on without her saying, "That's okay, I was the youngest in my family; I never made it to the dam."

And most youngests really don't make it to the dam in their own judgment unless they go into an entirely different field of work or lifestyle where they can succeed on their own terms. They tend to have fewer ambitions in life than their siblings and are the ones least likely to follow the family traditions. If left to their own devices, they often go into creative arts. Even when successful, they are not usually particularly serious about their careers. "Can you imagine," David Niven once said, "being wonderfully overpaid for dressing up and playing games?" Not surprisingly, many comedians are youngests: Billy Crystal, Eddie Murphy, Jim Carey, Martin Short.

If the older siblings have gone into business or professions, the youngest may become an artist or a farmer just to prevent comparisons. Youngests are often the most athletic in the family — especially if the older sibling does exceptionally well academically — and so find a career in sports, as did Joe Namath, youngest of five, or in some other physical endeavor. Though youngests may rebel against authority, they are more likely to be followers than leaders. If they happen to be in a leadership position, their followers will like them and their authority will not be taken too seriously. Of all the presidents of the United States, only four have been youngest sons. None of them was considered outstanding leaders. Two died within a few months of taking office and one was impeached. The fourth, Ronald Reagan, did finish his two terms. However, he displayed many youngest-son characteristics. He was affable but rather ineffectual, looked young for his age, did not work overly hard, and depended on others for guidance.

With their children they were trying to build a livable farm...during a worldwide depression... [which] made their work all the harder. I was the family baby and so had the privilege of watching the others without doing much myself....

Rudy Wiebe, "Father where are you?"

Youngests tend to be happiest in jobs that involve social interaction with people and in work that involves the practical and concrete rather than the abstract. They do well in music, languages, and the arts. They make better team workers than oldests, so are well suited to being orchestra members or repertory actors. They may do well in business because of their ability to relate well to others, but falter when required to train subordinates effectively or keep order. They don't want to or can't control or criticize others; instead, they look for praise and encouragement for themselves.

They often feel at a loss or panicky if they are in a highly responsible position. They lack the self-discipline required and often have difficulty making decisions since there was always someone older and wiser around to take care of things for them. They are not always reliable and don't usually worry about the details. "Act now and think later" may be the motto of youngests.

They continue to expect others (like a spouse or a co-worker) to solve their problems for them, whether they articulate that expectation or not. They may not trust themselves to handle difficult situations that arise. Sometimes they go to the opposite extreme of resenting and refusing all help, which can cause problems for them as employees.

They can be rebellious in their actions or their thinking. As Frank J. Sulloway found in his extensive research into birth order and scientific innovations, youngests were by far the most likely to propose (or support) radical new theories, such as Charles Darwin and his theory of evolution.

Youngests, who know what it's like to be the underdog often end up working on behalf of other powerless people in society, either politically or in settings such as nursing homes or halfway houses. Youngest son Mahatma Gandhi made a virtue of practicing civil disobedience in pursuit of justice.

Youngests tend to be risk-takers all their life and appear to be fearless in their attempt to prove themselves strong and capable, so are likely to take on dangerous jobs or invest in high-risk financial ventures.

f. TO THE PARENTS OF A YOUNGEST CHILD

Encourage your youngest child to be more independent, thoughtful, and self-reliant; involve the youngest in decision making. Praise minor accomplishments just as you did with your first child. Don't let the older children dominate or tease the youngest. Give plenty of affirmation for accomplishments and don't let him or her get away with goofing off too much.

Start reading early with your youngest and encourage intellectual development as much as other areas of endeavor. Don't assume the youngest is too little to be useful; give your youngest a fair share of household duties. Never compare the youngest to the older children.

Remember that the qualities of a youngest are not inherent genetically, but tend to go with the sibling position. As a parent, you are responsible for how that position gets understood and portrayed in the family. Look at your own expectations.

Make an effort to get new things for the youngest and let the youngest make decisions about what toys or clothes to buy, even if they aren't to your taste. Taking the youngest to a secondhand store to pick out clothes is preferable to handing down clothes without regard to the youngest's preferences. Or at the least, let the youngest choose what to keep from among the hand-me-downs.

Resist the temptation to hold on to the youngest when you fear being left on your own. Parents in Europe used to say about their youngest: "This one is for my old age." They meant that the youngest was expected to stay at home, not get married, and look after the parents in their old age. Guard against this attitude.

g. TO THE ADULT YOUNGEST CHILD

Even if you feel you are well-situated in life, check to see if you depend too much on others to take care of you. Try to learn to be more responsible, self-reliant, and "grown-up" in situations that call for it. Be aware that you may have some underlying resentment about being the littlest that is interfering with your current relationships.

Realize that there is no need to catch up with your older siblings now so stop comparing yourself to them. If you must measure your progress, try doing it against people younger than you. Accept the blame when appropriate, and clean up after yourself.

Make sure your work is people-oriented in some way. Try sharing the spotlight occasionally; ask other people about themselves and hold back your own stories for a while. But do keep on being your charming self and having a good time.

8
YOUNGEST SISTERS

I wish I could shimmy like my sister Kate

Popular song

a. YOUNGEST SISTER OF SISTERS

1. General characteristics

The youngest sister of sisters acts the youngest all her life. She tends to be spontaneous, cheerful, vivacious, playful, and adventurous no matter how old she is, which is exactly how Prince Andrew described his ex-wife Sarah, Duchess of York, the youngest of two girls.

The youngest sister of sisters may also be messy, capricious, and some would say, bratty at times. She may feel dominated by her older sister, but her mother is the person she feels closest to when growing up. She may have a rebellious adolescence, but then become more dependent as she gets older.

Her father may be disappointed that she wasn't a boy, particularly if she is the third or fourth daughter and the parents wanted a boy. He may react by ignoring her or by giving up and taking her on as his favored child anyway. As she grows up and becomes more attractive and feminine, he may turn against her to guard against his feelings of attraction, and suddenly become unreasonably strict about makeup, clothes, dating, and curfews. If her mother has had any feelings of jealousy about the father-daughter relationship, she is likely to support these restrictions. If her mother is a youngest sister, too, she is more likely to fight against father's restrictions.

Being the same sex as the siblings she follows makes it more difficult for the youngest sister to be different or stand out. She is seldom first at anything. As Sharon complained, her two older sisters would even get to have the first funerals and "no one will be left to come to mine."

Simone de Beauvoir wrote in her autobiography that the birth of her younger sister had been a disappointment to the family, because they had all wanted a boy: "Relegated to a secondary position, the little one felt almost superfluous. I had been a new experience for my parents: my sister found it much more difficult to surprise and astonish them...she was always being compared with me."

The youngest sister may try to be like her older sister at first, but since that rarely brings her the acclaim she seeks, she may rebel and do just the opposite of her older sister, whether it's what she really wants or not. At least it gets her some attention, which feels better than no attention at all, and it sends a clear message to the parents of "don't expect me to be like her."

She often has trouble making decisions — she doesn't want to have to choose one thing over another, she wants it all. Depending on her mood or the other circumstances of her childhood, she can be either very good to be around (when she is being fun-loving) or very bad (when she is being petulant).

The youngest of the family, Catherine and Lydia, were particularly frequent in these attentions; their minds were more vacant than their sisters', and when nothing better offered, a walk to Meryton was necessary to amuse their morning hours...

Jane Austen, *Pride and Prejudice*

Her approach to life is a very personal, self-centered one. She is used to getting attention by needing to be taken care of, whereas her sister gets attention by being a caretaker. She may be erratic in her beliefs and often seems to lack conviction. She can change her mind about her politics or her religion just because she is attracted to an adherent or dislikes an opponent of a particular point of view. She may be a radical of either the left or the right and usually appears to react to events out of emotion rather than logic.

"....the nickname Miss Baby...cut the ground from under my imperious stamping feet"....The happiness of Stevie's childhood grew out of many things....She was daring and gregarious.

Frances Spalding, *Stevie Smith: A Critical Biography*

Deaths in the family are a tragedy for her, especially the death of her father. If her mother dies, she can always turn to her older sisters as fill-ins, but she doesn't like it if her father remarries. The new mother, no matter who she is, will rarely measure up and will be seen as a competitor for father's attention.

If the older sister is a good student, the youngest sister is usually less interested in school than her sister and more interested in friends and social life. If her older sister has the "goodness" market cornered, she may be more defiant and become the family outcast or at least the unconventional one. The youngest sister has often had fewer parental expectations placed on her. As the youngest sister character in the old TV program "thirtysomething" said, after describing how much her parents expected of her older sister, "All I had to do was stay out of jail."

Sometimes, in families of three or more, the oldest and the youngest sister have a better relationship with each other than either of them do with the middle sister.

> I had made several attempts to snuff baby Amy in her cradle. Mother had repeatedly discovered me pouring glasses of water carefully into her face. So when Molly had appeared, Mother had led me to believe the new baby was a kind of present for me. Actually, the new baby displaced Amy. I liked everything about her — the strong purity of her cheeriness, bewilderment, outrage; her big dumb baldness...the works.
>
> Annie Dillard, *An American Childhood*

The youngest sister may fight against being babied, but still enjoy being indulged and invite it — sending double messages about her independence and dependence to those around her. Compared to her older siblings, her childhood may be carefree and happy and she a more delightful companion.

On occasion the youngest sister of sisters may actually outdo herself in trying to keep up with her sister, but then revert to babyish ways. The two sisters may continue to compete against each other as adults, each claiming to have the best husband, the best children, the best house, the best job, the best grandchildren, and so on.

Dreena was a 30-year-old youngest of three sisters. She came into therapy because she was "feeling at loose ends," and she didn't have "a clear direction." Throughout her life she had always had many interests and involvements and usually stood out at whatever she tried. She was extremely popular in school and was seen as having a "bright, open, and sparkling personality." But she never really felt as solid as others believed her to be. She had had many different jobs since college and was making a lot of money in her current job, but was starting to feel bored. This was a frequent pattern for her, and she had begun to think it was a problem.

Dreena also found her home boring. As much as possible, when she was young, she visited the homes of her friends, did things outside of the house and family, and just generally kept her distance. She had always felt the support of her parents in whatever she did, but there was no direction given. This was a problem for her. Their lack of direct input felt like lack of caring to her.

When she asked her parents about their experience of family, she found that they were both middle children who felt overwhelmed and dazzled by the abilities of their own youngest siblings. They both saw their youngest siblings as "stars" and had seen Dreena this way also. They felt just as dazzled by her and thought that they didn't have anything to offer her in terms of a direction in life.

Dreena realized that she had enjoyed being "dazzling" and that that, in itself, had become a goal for her. She was indeed a success at it. Now she faced the hard work of clarifying what else was important to her and what she believed in beyond her impact on people. She wanted to find something that would make the daily grind of a more "committed" and less dazzling life worthwhile.

2. As a spouse

The youngest sister of sisters can be competitive, especially with men, but she is also flirtatious and can play the feminine role to the hilt.

She may try to show up her older sister by being more attractive and is often sexually precocious. She is considered the most "feminine" of all women and is often more domestic than her sister. She is likely to marry before her sister does and have children sooner.

Although she attracts many men and they often flock around her, most of her relationships are short-lived; she is fickle and likes change. She wants to continue in her role of being the favored one with all the men in her life.

The easiest marriage for her is usually with an oldest brother of sisters who is able to handle her because he sees through her manipulative behavior. The oldest brother of brothers is an okay match for rank but not for gender since neither of them has had any experience of the opposite sex as peers. She may both depend on him too much and resent him "because he is too controlling." If they have children of both sexes — one for each of them — it might help bring them closer together.

A middle brother with younger sisters or an only child can also be satisfactory since they can handle a younger peer, though a male only child won't want much to do with household and child care duties, and neither will she.

Her poorest choice of husband is usually the youngest brother of brothers. They are likely to have conflicts since neither can nurture the other very well and neither is used to opposite-sex peers. For them, children only make things worse, as neither wants to play parent. If she marries a youngest brother of sisters and they happen to have a lot of money and don't have to work hard, they can have a most enjoyable life because both are good at having fun.

The youngest sister of sisters is more likely than most to seek a rich husband to satisfy her whims. But she may, just to be obstinate or to shock her family, choose a poor, incompetent man.

3. As a parent

No matter who her husband is, the youngest sister of sisters is not likely to be thrilled about mothering. She usually wants a lot of help with the children, if not from her husband or her mother, then from paid caregivers. In spite of this, she may be more suited to parenthood than her older sister. Since her parents were probably less tense with her, her parenting style is likely to be more laissez-faire and easygoing. Generally, she is a more liberal parent than an oldest sister, placing fewer restrictions on her children and protecting them less. She can be especially good with her children after they can take care of themselves and be her playmates.

4.   As a friend

The youngest sister of sisters is a joiner. She is happy in large groups and likes belonging to clubs and organizations so she can meet a lot of people. She is often a good raconteur, and friends find her entertaining.

Her best female friends are likely to be oldest sisters of sisters. They can have a very good relationship as long as they are not competing over a man. She may look to an oldest sister of brothers for guidance, but an oldest sister of brothers is not likely to be interested in having a close female friend. The youngest sister of brothers is another possibility, since she is, in effect, the oldest daughter in her family. Middle sisters with younger sisters may also offer some of the advantages of an oldest sister as a friend.

A female only child may also be a good friend, showing her how to be more independent, but not needing to control her. The more sisters the youngest sister has, the more she will be concerned with female friendships and the less with men and marriage, even though she may work hard at attracting men.

She is more likely than most to seek help with her personal problems from friends and especially from a paternal male therapist. However, she is not usually called upon to be helpful herself, and if she is, may be incapable of responding to the degree desired.

Olivia had often asked her friend Bertha for favors and help with things like last-minute babysitting. Bertha always seemed glad to help without expecting anything in return. Then one day she needed a babysitter at the last minute and asked Olivia. Olivia wasn't feeling well and said she couldn't do it. Bertha exploded angrily, and Olivia was hurt and confused. As the youngest, Olivia was much more accustomed to receiving help than giving it, and didn't think it would matter that she turned down her friend's request. Bertha, however, as an oldest, had found it risky to ask for help and never would have done so if she hadn't been in a jam. To take that risk and then be turned down for what she considered a trivial excuse was just too much.

5. At work

The youngest sister of sisters may do extremely well at work if an older man or woman is able to guide her in using her capabilities. Otherwise, she can be erratic in her work patterns. If there is some conflict at work, she can be stubborn and disagreeable even with her boss. She is usually the best producer if she is doing some highly skilled, but automatic job, such as being a secretary or radio announcer. She is sometimes creative, but often just flighty or unpredictable. She may resent a strong leader and close supervision, but she is not usually a leader herself. Recognition of her accomplishments is important to her.

Show business of one kind or another often attracts youngests, who may be actresses, singers, or dancers. Tina Turner, the youngest sister of sisters, is unusual only in the degree of her success and her longevity as a star. Working with the disadvantaged also attracts some of these youngests, who identify with the powerless in society.

6. To the parents of a youngest sister of sisters

Encourage her to pursue her own interests and do not compare her negatively to her older sister. Don't suggest that she be like her sister in any way, unless you want her to be just the opposite. Otherwise, follow the guidelines given for parents of all youngests in chapter 7.

7. To the adult youngest sister of sisters

Rather than focusing on your sister's competence and comparing yourself to her (which you may do more than you realize), concentrate on what you want for yourself and your own development. You will be happier when you take more responsibility for yourself and can be more direct and assertive in dealing with others. Don't keep trying to prove yourself. Be careful not to bite off more than you are willing to chew, so that you are able to follow through on your commitments.

b. YOUNGEST SISTER OF BROTHERS

1. General characteristics

The youngest sister of brothers is usually a congenial, warm, optimistic, fun-loving woman. She is often the special, favored one in her family, and she usually continues to be favored throughout her life. Things often just go her way without much effort on her part. She is usually cute, vivacious, and popular.

When opera star Beverly Sills (née Belle Silverman) was born, her father said to her mother, "We already have two sons.... Belle is our dessert."

Like other youngests, this one often scores lower on intelligence tests and usually has less drive to achieve than others in her family. The family's hopes and resources for achievement often go to her older brother. Living in his shadow means she receives less pressure to succeed but also little encouragement to pursue her own goals.

 My parents' ambitions were focused largely on me.

Pierre Berton, writing about his younger sister in *Starting Out, 1920-1947*

The lack of parental expectations can be a relief and often gives the youngest sister of brothers a more carefree attitude toward life. The negative side of this (which she may not experience as a problem when young) is that she isn't encouraged to pursue any other career except that of being a wife and mother, although this is changing as attitudes toward work and marriage change.

If all the emphasis is placed on making the older brother a success while ignoring the needs of the youngest sister, she may feel inadequate or resentful, especially if she has some talent that is being overlooked. She may develop an underlying anger at men and try to compete with them. If she has several older brothers, she may envy men and be dissatisfied with her own life, especially if her mother expected a great deal of household help from her and none from her brothers. This youngest may direct her rebellion against society by refusing to fit into the standard feminine role. Not only can she never catch up, but she can never be a boy anyway, so why try to accomplish anything?

Some youngest sisters of brothers may be tomboys simply because they played with their brothers and learned how to be hardy and brave. Some may become daredevils just to prove they can keep up with and be as good as a boy. This usually puts them in good standing in the male world, but they seldom know how to take advantage of this to further their careers.

The youngest sister of brothers doesn't usually place too much importance on possessions, but she often ends up having many — they just seem to come to her without her making any effort. She may not always be financially responsible, however.

2. As a spouse

Usually, men are attracted by the good looks and compatibility of the youngest sister of brothers. They tend to flock around and chase her. She, in turn, is very fond of men. She wants a man she can look up to and admire as she did her brother. However, she doesn't want to be dominated by him. Ballerina Margot Fonteyn spoke for many women in this birth position when she wrote in her autobiography, "My brother Felix, three years older than me, was always my hero. He had my unfailing devotion and respect from the very beginning, excepting only the day he threw the worm at me...."

The youngest sister of brothers is also the woman who is most likely to attract older or married men, let them ruin their marriages for the sake of winning her attention, and then reject them later. The pattern of Elizabeth Taylor's relationships with men reflects this.

The more brothers this youngest has, the more difficult it is for her to settle for just one man in her life. In extreme circumstances, because she knows how to please men, a youngest sister of brothers becomes promiscuous and perhaps a prostitute. In the latter case, she was likely to have been sexually abused by her brothers or her father.

However, if her older brother was secure and treated her well, she usually marries happily and considers her husband her prize possession. She may be loyal to him no matter what, even if he turns out to be a jerk. She may at times be too submissive, though she can also be selfish. She usually has several male friends besides her husband. These relationships are usually platonic, on her part if not theirs, and she uses these men as mentors for her life and sometimes her work.

The best matrimonial match for the youngest sister of brothers is often an oldest brother of sisters. He tends to be comfortable with women and knows how to cater to a charming one. She is used to males who are older in rank and knows how to charm them. She is pretty secure with men and is the most likely woman to make her best match.

She is usually smart enough to stay away from an oldest brother of brothers, who may be attracted to her, but not overwhelmed by her charms. A youngest brother of sisters is usually a difficult match also, because they may both compete for the favored position they were used to as children. The youngest brother of brothers is often the most difficult match since they both want to be taken care of and, in addition, he may have no patience with her femaleness.

A middle brother with a younger sister may be okay, especially if there are many years between him and his older siblings. An only child whose father was an oldest of sisters and taught his son how to treat women may work, but there can be conflict over the "starring" role since they are both only children of a sort.

If her husband dies, she will be crushed, though others will rush in to console her. She has great difficulty with the death of any loved one, though in early childhood the greatest loss is her mother. Later in life, the death of a favorite brother or her father is the hardest for her to take.

If the youngest sister has many older brothers, she may not be able to settle for one man at a time. She may choose to stay at home with her doting parents and the brothers who come home often for family visits.

3. As a parent

The youngest sister of brothers is more often the one who has been taken care of in her family than the one who did the caretaking. In her autobiography, Beverly Sills writes, "....my brothers did most of the looking out — I was the baby of the family. Sidney, being the eldest, was the designated heir apparent. The family called him `Doc' — they picked out his profession before Sidney could walk — and he resembled my father and watched over me in much the same way Papa did." As a result, the woman in this birth position may have children only to please her husband, but she is usually a good mother, especially with boys — so good that her sons may become too attached to her, even though she will teach the children to adore their father as she does.

She can be a good companion to her children. She usually enjoys her sons the most and will give them quite a bit of autonomy, sometimes putting them into the big brother role with herself.

4. As a friend

Although she makes friends easily, the youngest sister of brothers is not particularly interested in female friends. She doesn't look for them, and if they seek her out, she may innocently take their men away. Women are often jealous of her even without cause. When she does have female friends, she usually gets along best with a youngest sister of sisters. They understand each other and there is less competition for men.

Partly because of her "lucky" life and partly because of all her helpful male admirers, she rarely seeks help from female friends or in counseling.

5. At work

The youngest sister of brothers is not usually a career woman. She would rather devote herself to her husband, his work, and their children. When she does work, she is best as an employee with a male supervisor. She is usually as loyal to her boss as she is to her husband and does everything necessary to do a good job for him. She gets along well with all the men at work. She isn't as friendly to the women, and they may resent her without quite knowing why.

She often goes into acting, and with the right male directors can excel in it as a professional. Dame Peggy Ashcroft is a good example. Shirley Temple, the youngest sister of two much older brothers, cornered the market on cuteness and stole the hearts of her co-actors as well as her audiences.

This birth order position makes a good political wife in the conventional sense of supporting her husband and winning votes for him. In this setting, she will have no ambitions for herself. Betty Ford illustrated this characteristic most ably.

The youngest sister of brothers has more handicaps in fields such as teaching. As a counselor she may run into trouble with male patients because she is too understanding of them and as a therapist she lacks perception about them.

6. To the parents of a youngest sister of brothers

Give your daughter as much encouragement as you give your son to develop interests and career goals. These days, marriage is not automatically going to be in her future, and even if she does marry, she is likely to have a career as well. Be careful that the focus of your attention and energy is not just on the boys, or she will get the message that she has to be "one of the boys" to get attention.

7. To the adult youngest sister of brothers

Look for ways to fulfill yourself that don't involve a man. Remember that women long outlive men and you will likely be alone for many years. Make sure you have interests of your own and female friends for company.

Pay attention to how much you rely on men to make the decisions or set directions for you, rather than using your own wisdom.

c. YOUNGEST SISTER OF SISTERS AND BROTHERS

Depending on the age differences and who is just before her in birth order, this woman will share characteristics with either the youngest sister of sisters or the youngest sister of brothers. However, she may also be more feminine and submissive than the youngest sister of sisters and more ambitious than the youngest sister of brothers.

She is less likely to tolerate bad behavior in a man, but usually relates well to both men and women, especially those who are her seniors.

Carlotta was the attractive youngest sister of two girls and a boy. At 26, she had become unhappy with the way she dealt with men and wanted to change her style of relating. She said that she "let them think that they are in control" while believing at the same time that she could "wrap them around my little finger," just as she had always done with her father and brother.

She ended up losing interest in the men because they could so easily be manipulated. She lost respect for them just as she had lost respect for her father. But she had also lost respect for herself for using her charm and her good looks to get her way. She started working on being more direct in asking for what she wanted in a relationship and dealing with men in a more open, adult manner, especially in serious situations. For example, with her boyfriends (and with her boss) she stopped making indirect requests using her cute, coy, seductive little girl voice, hinting at "what would be nice." She assumed a more grown-up stance and adult voice and asked specifically for what she wanted. If they said "no," rather than have a tantrum she would then look for other ways to accomplish her goal. She no longer felt dependent on them doing things for her. She found this much more satisfying, although she still enjoyed being the "cute youngest" at times.

9
YOUNGEST BROTHERS

When I am grown to man's estate
I shall be very proud and great,
And tell the other girls and boys
Not to meddle with my toys.

Robert Louis Stevenson, *Looking Forward*

a. YOUNGEST BROTHER OF BROTHERS

1. General characteristics

The youngest brother of brothers is often like the daring young man on the flying trapeze. He is headstrong, capricious, and often rebellious. He longs to be free, yet he is lost without a structure to rebel against and may be very dependent on others.

If the oldest brother is treated as the heir apparent, the second son, or the third or whoever is the youngest son, doesn't have a well-defined niche for himself. Sometimes he becomes mother's pet, as was the case with poet W. H. Auden, whose two older brothers left him behind at home with mother, who seemed to want his company. He was, he wrote in a poem, "the

Happy-Go-Lucky," the spoilt third son. As with many youngests, he was always convinced "that in any company I am the youngest person present."

More often, however, the youngest brother is just the less significant one of "the boys." His older brother has always been there — as mentor and guide or as boss and persecutor. If they have been primarily playmates, which happens more often when there are three or four years between them, the relationship may be rewarding and close.

Younger brothers are often compared unfavorably to the "good" older brother and expected to be like him. For instance, younger brothers are often less comfortable in the academic setting of school than the older brother and learn better in other ways. But parents and teachers alike think that if one brother is a good student, the other should be also.

Kermit [older brother] is such a well-behaved boy in contrast to Arthur.

Arthur Miller's elementary school teacher, quoted in *Timebends*

To maintain his individuality, the younger brother of brothers usually tries to be as unlike his older brother as possible. "I'm not like Norm," he will assert, "and don't want to be." If his older brother is messing up, then the youngest may decide to be the "good" one or the achiever as a way to compete. But if the older brother follows the usual older brother path of achievement, the youngest brother often tries other ways to win affirmation — as a joker or a troublemaker, perhaps. Many comedians are youngests or near-youngests, such as Walter Matthau, youngest of two boys; Billy Crystal, youngest of three boys; and Bob Hope, fifth of seven boys.

Actor Dustin Hoffman admits to being the black sheep in his family in contrast to his straight-A student older brother. Dustin was always the clown who did things like altering the line in his role as Tiny Tim in a school play, "God bless us all, goddamn it." His brother had the first professional acting role in the family, and it wasn't until he gave up acting that Dustin pursued it.

This youngest can be carefree and good-natured when things are going well, and he is often a mystic or a romantic. He is also often unpredictable: he may be in a jolly mood one moment and a foul mood the next. He may excel at something one time and fail another time. He doesn't usually plan ahead, but lives for the moment and the gratification of his immediate desires, which makes him flexible and spontaneous most of the time, but also hard to satisfy.

...my inability to forgo, to wait until a wish could be fulfilled; I had to have what I wanted at once...my life consisted of explosions of desires that could not wait to be satisfied, in contrast to my brother's self-control and responsibility.

Arthur Miller, *Timebends*

He may also avoid doing necessary tasks or leave unpleasant things until the last minute hoping that they'll go away or that someone else will take care of them. Since his older brother often "helped" him or took over an activity if it was going too slowly, the youngest brother may often feel helpless and then depressed.

Nate was a youngest brother who got a lot of attention and affection from his oldest brother by being dependent, uncertain, and somewhat bumbling. As an adult, he had chosen a more ascetic lifestyle compared to his brother's materialistic and "successful" style. However, Nate sought acceptance by ostensibly agreeing with his older brother's ideas. Whenever he disagreed, he just kept quiet and withdrew. He said he had a "sneaky" kind of anger. He found that he was not being himself with his brother or with other people because it felt too scary for him to voice his own opinions. He was afraid he would lose the support and caring that he thought he needed. When Nate began to stop going along automatically with everything his brother said, his brother was at first puzzled and then angry. But Nate found that he could survive the anger and that his brother got over being angry and still wanted to be close. Nate discovered he could even say things that made his older brother rethink his position. They eventually established a more adult-to-adult relationship.

What this younger brother had to learn was that he could stand on his own feet and did not need the support and help of his older brother to get through life, although he still valued the relationship. He found that as he calmly asserted himself and expressed his own thoughts his brother began to respect him more.

As a child, the youngest brother of brothers rarely has a chance to express his anger directly and get anywhere with his older, smarter, stronger brother. He may become a whiner or throw tantrums out of frustration. As an adult, if things are not going well, he usually just leaves; he doesn't like losing.

Franz continually found himself unable to argue effectively and convince his older brother Wilhelm of anything. Although he was 45 years old, Franz felt that Wilhelm treated him as though he were still 5, and Franz often acted as though he were 5 when he was with Wilhelm. His frustration at not being taken seriously sometimes made him incoherent. His own doubts about himself in comparison to his brother made him back down, even when he felt strongly about something. He said the whole relationship was summed up in a Trivial Pursuit game that he and his brother and their wives played one night. The two men were teamed against the two women. Almost every time it was their turn to answer a question, Franz knew and suggested the right answer, but Wilhelm disagreed with it, and Franz, in his insecurity, went along with Wilhelm's answer. When the correct answer turned out to be Franz's first suggestion, Franz got furious and practically stamped his feet. But each time it was their turn, he gave in again, was right again, and got angry again. He finally couldn't stand it any more and just refused to play any longer, blaming it on Wilhelm.

It is common for the younger brother of brothers to find it difficult to be calm and to get agitated easily in his effort to keep up with his brother or to prove a point. He thinks (and as a child he may be right) that people aren't listening to him or taking him seriously. Yet he also may have trouble sitting still to listen to others or to discuss things.

He tends to be a daring, high-stakes risk-taker. He has a talent for causing trouble, then getting out of the way while someone else gets the blame. He may knock down his brother's Lego creation and then cry for mother when his brother pushes him away. He may have trouble all through life taking responsibility for himself. He may always look for others to blame for his problems.

He is usually given things more freely than the older brother is, without being taught to take responsibility for them. He often unintentionally squanders his money when older.

2.   As a spouse

The youngest brother of brothers is generally gregarious in groups of men, but shy with women. He hasn't had much contact with peers of the opposite sex, so he will not really understand them — he may even be a little afraid of them. Sometimes he will be too polite, which makes him appear awkward, or he will act the clown around women.

His mother is very important to him and if he feels good about his childhood experiences with her, he may want a wife who will provide the same kind of home for him.

The oldest sister of brothers is usually the easiest match for him, particularly if she is the more maternal type and stays behind the scenes. He will let her control his life if she does it unobtrusively. He may not ask for help, but will be unhappy if it is not forthcoming.

A middle sister who has younger brothers is also a possible choice. The most difficult marriage is usually with a youngest sister of sisters. Neither of them knows how to handle the opposite sex and neither of them wants to be responsible for running a household or parenting, or for the decision making that is part of marriage. However, if there are few outside pressures in their life, they can enjoy the playfulness in each other.

3.   As a parent

Having children is often a strain for the youngest brother of brothers; he doesn't like giving up his place as the youngest. He usually has little tolerance for the work of taking care of an infant and may resent the time his wife spends with the baby. Once his children are beyond infancy, he may be a good companion since he finds it easy to play at their level, especially if they are boys. His difficulty is in setting effective and consistent limits, exercising consistent discipline, and nurturing their emotional needs.

4.   As a friend

Male friends are usually more important to the youngest brother of brothers than wife or children, and he is likely to be easily swayed by his peers. His best male friend is often an oldest brother of brothers, though he may find he has much in common with other youngest brothers. No matter who his friends are, he counts on getting help from them when he needs it.

He wants to be understood, but he has trouble understanding others. When others leave him or die, he is confused by it. The loss of his mother is the most painful one; the loss of his wife is not felt as deeply unless she was a strong mother figure for him.

Since he likes being taken care of by mentors and mothers, he is likely to seek the help of a counselor and enjoy therapy, though he may become too dependent on the counselor. A less skilled counselor could easily be lured into being an older sibling for him, giving him a lot of advice rather than guiding him in growing up.

5.   At work

The youngest brother of brothers often works best when he is competing with another worker or has a superior watching him. He tends to be a follower at work or else he comes up with off-beat, and sometimes unacceptable, suggestions for change. Given a mentor or wife who takes care of him and creates opportunities for him, he may excel, especially in scientific or artistic work.

His unconventional approach to life helps him see common things in uncommon ways. He may see new needs and new ways of fulfilling them and is often ingenious and creative. His problem is in getting others to give his ideas serious consideration.

Inventor Thomas Edison was the seventh son in his family and had only three months of formal education. His teacher called him "addled," and he left school at age 13. He was sloppy around the house and often pulled stunts on the servants — such as feeding them worms because he thought that it would make them fly. Yet his unconventional approach to solving puzzles led to brilliant solutions.

Since the youngest son isn't able to compete intellectually with an older brother when he is growing up, he often turns to physical activities, such as sports or dance, or creative activities, such as art or acting, as a way to be different and win applause. Youngest brother Paul Newman has done that successfully both as an actor and a race-car driver. He also works on behalf of the underprivileged.

Ronald Reagan as a child was often in fistfights and was picked up by the police. He later followed the athletic path of playing football and being a lifeguard before turning to sports announcing, acting, and then politics. He did, however, lack true leadership skills and depended heavily on his wife and advisors.

The youngest brother tends to be fearless and will do anything that brings attention or acclaim, whether taking a canoe over a waterfall or trying a daring and radical artistic innovation.

Tony, the baby — strange and beautiful waif — was a brooding, imaginative solitary...he suffered from being the odd one of three...he was always either running to keep up with the rest of us or sitting alone in the mud. He drew like an artist, wouldn't read or write, sang and danced, was quite without fear...was the one true visionary amongst us....

Laurie Lee, *I Can't Stay Long*

He may strive for fame to prove he can be as good as the older brother. In some cases this means he will do the opposite of what his brother does even if it means being a failure when his brother is a success.

If put in a leadership position, the youngest brother of brothers is often not very good in it. He can be erratic and inconsistent in the way he treats subordinates. Females working for him have to pamper him and act in awe of him to please him.

He can be generous with those under him, and he doesn't push people to achieve. Those who are able to take responsibility without threatening him will end up doing all the work for him while he gets the credit.

If his superior is male, a good supervisor, and likes him, the youngest brother of brothers will be a good worker and will tend to idolize the older man. If his superior is unjust in any way or does not appreciate his charm, the youngest brother may become a troublemaker at work and undercut the work of others.

His resentment of authority can lead him to be a revolutionary hero during a conflict, such as Davy Crockett was at the Alamo, but in peacetime he may merely be a thug. Many assassins are youngest sons — John Wilkes Booth, Lee Harvey Oswald, and Sirhan Sirhan, for example. He opposes anything that seems to him like dictatorship (remembering his older brother's power over him) unless the dictator is very good to him.

Youngest brothers often become entertainers, salesmen, musicians, ophthalmologists, or technical specialists of some kind. As mentioned earlier, youngest brothers who become scientists are much more likely to create or support radical new theories or innovations than oldest brothers are.

If they become teachers or therapists, these youngests don't worry very much about their students or clients and may be more concerned about being liked than about helping others learn or improve themselves.

6. To the parents of a youngest brother of brothers

Don't make comparisons between the two boys or put labels on them like "the scholar and the clown." Make sure that neither you nor others take responsibility for the youngest's actions or decisions because "he doesn't seem able to handle them." He won't be able to handle them if you keep doing for him what he could do for himself. Listen to what he has to say and expect him to listen to you as well. Let him deal with the consequences of his behavior without your rescuing him.

7. To the adult youngest brother of brothers

You may want to practice taking the initiative more often, being more open with your ideas, and being more responsible for their execution. You may also need to work at improving your verbal skills in order to be more competitive in the job market. Remember that your brother no longer has power over you and is no longer your keeper. You can and should stand on your own two feet and make your own unique contributions to the world.

b. YOUNGEST BROTHER OF SISTERS

1. General characteristics

The youngest brother of sisters is usually taken care of by women all his life. In most cases, this is just fine with him.

His older sisters may be either loving and protective or domineering and bossy, and sometimes both. If his sisters were too domineering, he may react by being passive and wishy-washy or by being difficult and rebellious.

The greater the age difference, the more likely his oldest sister is to be like a mother to him and perhaps treat him like one of her dolls. He usually takes on his father's attitude toward his mother and sisters, so he needs his father around to support him and model both assertiveness and kindness.

When he is young, this boy is more often considered a sissy than other boys, but as an adolescent he may try to break away from his female-dominated household by playing a macho role or going through a period of stormy rebellion. If he was allowed to be assertive and was not babied too much, he usually has high self-esteem and takes it for granted that women like him and will cater to him.

Marlon Brando was pampered by his mother, who was more permissive with him than with his two older sisters and let him virtually take over the role of the man in the house, even while his father was there. He once told his father, who was also named Marlon, to change his name. His father defensively replied, "I had it first."

As a child, the youngest brother of sisters was probably doted upon — not only because he was the youngest, but also because he was unique (being male) and probably desired by the parents. (Surveys indicate that most parents want at least one boy and will keep trying if they have girls to start with.) Because of his special position, he never has to try very hard to distinguish himself in either accomplishments or opinions. He tends to follow the guidance of his sisters in forming his values, and he usually has few definite political opinions or religious beliefs — he goes along with his family.

In many families, however, the older sisters are relegated to the background and the youngest child, because he's male, is treated more like an oldest. The youngest brother of sisters in this situation is usually quick to take advantage of the situation and grasp the power. Pierre Trudeau and Abraham Lincoln, both the youngest brother of one sister, might fall into this category.

The youngest brother of sisters tends to be unrealistic about himself and others and may have frequent changes of mood, though he is usually a genial sort. If the family setting has been a good one, he will stay close to his sisters all his life.

In the biography *Let the Trumpet Sound,* Martin Luther King, Jr. is quoted as saying that he had a "childhood desire to keep up with" his older sister. When he was five, she ran to the front of the church one morning in response to a call to membership. He ran after her to prevent her from getting ahead of him and thus began his career in the church. He seemed to combine the characteristics of an oldest (as oldest male) and youngest (which he was). He was a serious student, but "loquacious and debonair in his social life." He called himself an "ambivert" — both an extrovert and an introvert.

If a youngest brother feels his sisters are much stronger than he is, he may feel incompetent as a man and fear rejection by women. If too dominated by his sisters and mother, he may seek passive women that he can dominate to prove himself. In this case, he may feel that his father let him down and, therefore, may harbor some resentment toward males in authority or expect more from them than they can give.

2. As a spouse

The more sisters the youngest brother has, the more difficult it is for him to settle for just one mate. However, he is usually happy to marry and will have plenty of women to choose from. Women are usually eager to please him even though he doesn't always give much of himself to them.

His wife has to be willing to take care of him — perhaps devote her life to him — while he treats her with benevolent indifference and goes about living his own life. If she makes too many demands on him, he is likely to have a tantrum. He doesn't usually reveal much of himself, as he has learned to protect his inner feelings from the older, stronger females in his life, especially if they have ridiculed or criticized him for his thoughts.

His passivity can create problems for both him and his wife; the marriage will improve when he learns to assert himself with women.

Reg, the youngest brother of two sisters, had been married to Caroline for 17 years but had been having affairs for 15 of those years. He had not been happy in his marriage. He admired Caroline's abilities as a parent and homemaker, but he was intimidated by her (an oldest sister of a sister) and was unable to open up with her about his feelings in order to work on changing the marriage. Because his parents had focused their ambitions on him rather than on his older sisters, he functioned in the business world like an oldest child and appeared to be in control. But emotionally he felt small and weak. He sought therapy when he met a woman he thought was the one and only for him. He was afraid to leave his wife and he was afraid he would lose this woman if he didn't leave his wife. However, he wasn't able to take the therapy seriously. He could not look at his family history and the role he was playing now. His marriage ended, he lost confidence in his abilities as a business manager and was fired, and his "one true love" stopped seeing him after he left his wife.

The youngest brother of sisters usually feels most comfortable with an oldest sister of brothers, who is good at taking care of little boys and may be willing to be the woman behind the great man for him — whether he does anything great in the world or not.

The oldest sister of sisters is able to do the caretaking for him, but she may resist giving up her own interests for his sake. The youngest sister of sisters may be more flighty and irresponsible than he is and fail to appreciate his maleness. Ronald Reagan's only child wife was a good match for him, providing him with structure and order and a home that was for Reagan "like coming out of the cold into a warm firelit room."

No matter who the youngest brother of brothers marries, his sisters may still try to take care of him, which he may like. He may even be jealous of their husbands and try to come between them in some way.

In any case, he is usually nice to all his women without working too hard at pleasing them. He isn't an especially good provider, and may do best if his wife takes charge of the finances so he doesn't throw his money away. They may struggle over his apparent lack of ambition.

3.   As a parent

If he has children, the youngest brother of sisters may consider them an intrusion. He may turn to his work or other outside interests to escape — at least until they are older, when he may begin to find pleasure in them.

A son may be perceived as a rival, so he often does better with daughters. He is just as happy not to have children, and his wife may have the whole burden of parenting any children they do have — at least until the children are old enough to share in his interests. If his wife is another youngest, neither of them may want the responsibility of parenting and they often do best without children. If they have children anyway, he may well end the marriage.

Philip had three older sisters. He was married to Roseanne who had the characteristics of an only child because her one sister was seven years younger. However, Roseanne's mother was the oldest sister of a brother so Roseanne learned from her how to take care of men.

In the early days of their marriage, Philip was happy with the attention Roseanne paid to him and she worked hard at being a devoted wife and mother in the conventional sense. Philip would have liked other women in his life, but he settled for monogamy while things were going well. As their sons grew older, Roseanne began to resent how little Philip helped with the parenting and other household responsibilities.

After Roseanne started her own business with two women friends, she had less and less time to devote to the family. Feeling both abandoned and freed, Philip began having affairs.

Roseanne resented this and fought with Philip about it, but still wanted to stay married for the sake of the two boys. However, Philip felt little attachment to the boys and eventually moved out. He kept in touch with Roseanne, but rarely contacted his sons — it was as if they didn't even exist. This was not really how he felt, but because he had not been very involved with the boys as a parent, he felt ill at ease alone with them. He dealt with his feelings of inadequacy by keeping his distance.

4. As a friend

Male friends may be important to the youngest brother of sisters, but he is often not particularly popular with other males. As a child he may be shy and not feel comfortable joining in the boisterous, rowdy play of other boys.

The more sisters he has, the more difficult it usually is for him to make friends with men. Other men often think the youngest brother of sisters is spoiled or arrogant, which in fact he often is. He may, for example, expect his friends to clean up any mess — actual or metaphorical — that he leaves behind.

The youngest brother of brothers is usually his best choice for a male friend as they are less likely to offend each other with their erratic behavior. His best friendships may be with older, motherly women. He would make good use of therapy with that kind of woman, for instance.

When he loses family or friends, he doesn't usually experience much grief; those who are left take care of him so that he doesn't see his own well-being threatened by a loss. As a child, he will be most affected by the loss of his mother or a favorite sister.

5. At work

The youngest brother of sisters is a capable worker, but not always willing to make much of an effort.

He may deliberately choose work that is traditionally non-female, such as auto mechanics or engineering, to prove his maleness and separateness from sisters. If he is excited by his job and he is talented, he can become an expert in his field, especially if working on his own. If he has a woman at home taking good care of him, he may lose himself in his work. However, he may have difficulty meeting deadlines and staying on the right track. He works best in areas that have rigid job descriptions and don't require self-motivation. He may work hard at things that are his own particular interest, but they are often not seen as important by others. He usually does well in the fields of writing, science, dentistry, and entertainment. Fred Astaire, Warren Beatty, and comedian Gene Wilder are all youngest brothers of a sister.

6. To the parents of a youngest brother of sisters

As with other youngests, give him a lot of opportunities to think for himself, make his own decisions, and take responsibility for meeting his goals. Don't step in, or let his sisters do so, when he looks confused or uncertain or overwhelmed. Let him deal with the situation and face the consequences of his mistakes or reap the rewards of his triumphs by himself.

7. To the adult youngest brother of sisters

Your greatest challenge in life may be to risk being open and straight with women, even though you see them as the source of your security. If you don't confront the important women in your life when necessary, you may have trouble making any headway in your life emotionally.

c. YOUNGEST BROTHER OF BROTHERS AND SISTERS

The youngest brother of both brothers and sisters is less competitive and rebellious than the youngest brother of brothers, and he is better able to find a responsible woman to take care of him. He is more at ease with other males than the youngest brother of sisters and more likely to be one of the boys and less involved in the single-minded pursuit of work or a hobby.

Poet Samuel Taylor Coleridge, the "darling" youngest of ten children, repeatedly looked for nurturing from both women and men as an adult. He even sought wisdom from his own eldest son. Despite his masterpiece, "The Ancient Mariner," he was known for his inability to finish projects he started and was physically restless as well, often dashing out to walk in the mountains completely unprepared.

Andrew and his girlfriend, Camille, had been dating for more than three years when Camille began pressuring Andrew to get married. They argued about it constantly and finally sought therapy to work it out. He kept saying things would be fine if she would forget about getting married — that "marriages just ruin good relationships." She also wanted them to move to another city 50 miles away where she thought she could start a little business that would do well. He refused outright. He said he would never move from where he was living at the time. He explained, and his older brother and sisters agreed, that he just couldn't tolerate either a marriage or a move. He said he put his roots down deep and he didn't like changes in his life.

As he talked about it in therapy, Andrew was able to trace his stubbornness and emotional distancing patterns back to his childhood in the family. He had frequently been compared to his "more responsible, competent, successful, and obedient" older brother by his parents, while his older sisters took care of and "coddled" him. He reacted to the comparisons by getting more and more rebellious and taking the stand of "no one can make me do anything." His parents had taken this as a challenge and tried even harder to get him to "be more like your brother." The more they did this, and the more they punished him for his disobedience, the more rebellious he became. He was supported in his rebellion by his sisters who saw him as a victim of the parents and who dealt with their own feelings about their older brother by focusing on "helping" Andrew and going along with his wants. So he learned not to even consider doing something that someone else wanted and expected the women in his life to support him in his rebellion.

Meanwhile, Camille was helped to look at her pattern of emotional pursuit and to evaluate how well it was working for her. She decided she was banging her head against a brick wall and stopped talking about marriage and moving. Andrew breathed a sigh of relief and things calmed down in the relationship. But Camille then began to look at her life separately from Andrew and decided that she had to pursue her own goals, whether he was going to be with her or not. She said she was sad about it, but she had to get on with her life; she made plans to move to the new city and to start her new business there. Andrew joked with her about these plans and thought she was just "talking" — until the day she moved.

Camille's business demanded so much of her time that she started working harder on making it a success than she worked on making the relationship a success. Whenever Andrew and Camille had any time together from then on, it was because Andrew initiated it. Eventually he proposed that they get married and he move to where she was living. Two years after the wedding, Camille was still pursuing her goals instead of pursuing Andrew, and he was learning that being flexible and making changes in his life did not mean giving up his identity.

10
BETWIXT AND BETWEEN: MIDDLE CHILDREN

Tenants of life's middle state,
Securely plac'd between the small and great.

William Cowper, "Tirocinium"

a. GENERAL CHARACTERISTICS

Middle children, whether the second child of three or one of several in-between children in a family of four or more, are difficult to describe. They can have the characteristics of all other birth orders or none. They may be lost in the crowd or develop a particular kind of prominence as a result of being a middle.

While there may be fewer and fewer middle children in coming generations as family size shrinks (the North American average is currently 1.3 children per family down from 4.8 in the early fifties), many of today's middle-aged and older adults are middle children.

Corroborating the idea that middles are often just left out is the fact that fewer research studies have been done on middles than on any other birth order position.

Middles are difficult to pin down because they are at once younger siblings to the children they follow and older siblings to the children who follow them. So they often end up being confused about their identity. As a result, many do not develop distinctive traits. They are, after all, not particularly special in the family in the way the first-born child is by virtue of being the first or in the way the last-born is by virtue of being the baby.

In one study of families of three or more children, the oldest child and the youngest child were the clear favorites of the parents. Middle children often joke about the family photo album or home videos that have 3,000 pictures of the first child, 100 of the first and middle together, 10 of the middle alone, and 2,000 of the last child.

Another experience middle children commonly have when looking at the family pictures is the image of themselves in the hand-me-downs and their older and younger siblings in smart new clothes.

 I was the seventh of nine children. When you come from that far down you have to struggle to survive.

Robert F. Kennedy, *Handbook of 20th Century Quotations*

Middle children never experience having their parents all to themselves and getting as much attention as the oldest child. While they benefit from the calmer, more relaxed atmosphere that accompanies later births in the family, they are soon displaced by the new baby.

The middle child then is forced to compete for attention with an older, smarter, stronger sibling and a younger, cuter, more dependent sibling. As a result, the middle child may vacillate between trying to be grown-up and good like the older sibling and trying to be helpless and cute like the baby, with no true sense of his or her own uniqueness.

One middle child recalled her parents introducing the children to strangers by saying, "This is June, our oldest, and John, our baby, and Jane." Just plain Jane.

The birth of the youngest baby is usually more threatening to the middle child than to the oldest sibling, who has been through it all before and who, by this time, may be old enough to enjoy a baby in the house. In that case, a bond may develop between the oldest and youngest that leaves out the middle child.

I was caught between Joan, who had clearly taken my place as chief baby, and my brother, whose stature I could not begin to match.

Arthur Miller, *Timebends*

Middle children, since they have neither the rights of the oldest child nor the favors of the youngest, often feel that life is unfair. They are too young for the good stuff and too old to get away with anything. They are sensitive to being left out or slighted as an adult. This particular sensitivity is often one part in the mix that makes them good negotiators for arriving at fair settlements.

Another result of this indeterminate position is that middle children tend to be less capable of taking the initiative or thinking independently. In general, they are the lowest achievers academically and the least likely in their family to go to university. To avoid failure, they may not stick with anything too long and may try to set up conditions where others can't perform well so they will feel inadequate too. If there is an area where the oldest child does not do well, the next child may take over in that area and be a perfectionist in it, while being lax or negligent in everything else.

On the positive side, if the parents are worriers, middle children receive less of it than the oldest, who is closely monitored during all the "first attempts," and the youngest, who is so helpless and vulnerable. They catch less of the anxiety that goes with this worrying and are freer to develop naturally, whereas the other birth order positions have their development affected by anxiety. In some families, the middles think they are lucky to have this lowered amount of attention and worry.

Middle children are also less pressured to succeed than an oldest child. They quickly learn that other people (two parents and an older sibling) are usually around to help them when they need it. Since they were never alone with their parents, they feel less betrayed when the next child is born than the oldest did when the middle child was born.

Even though they may be bossed around by the oldest sibling, middle children have the opportunity to do some bossing of their own with the youngest. They often shift allegiances between older and younger siblings, and as adults their convictions may not be as firm as those of their older and younger siblings.

However, in their attempts to feel important, middle children may become competitive, though they may not compete head-on with the rest of the family. For example, if they belong to a family of achievers, they might choose to become destructive. They may become self-destructive by eating or drinking too much, for example, or they may become socially destructive by becoming a gang member or a criminal (like Al Capone, the middle child of seven boys, who wanted to make a name for himself and "be somebody"). The closer the middle child is in age to the older sibling, the stronger the competitive instincts, especially when the children are the same sex. Field Marshal Bernard Montgomery, who followed one of his older brothers by one year, was described by the oldest brother as "the bad boy in the family, mischievous by nature and individualist by character," according to the biography *Montgomery of Alamein*. His two older brothers had a tutor from England, but Bernard had to go to a girl's infant school with his younger sister. He never forgot or forgave the unfairness of this.

While middle children are usually more responsible than youngest children, they have more problems than either youngest or oldest. They lack the authority of the oldest and the spontaneity of the youngest. They may be introverted. Grace Kelly, a middle child, was shy, quiet, and sickly as a child. Even middle child Johnny Carson is said to be reserved, withdrawn, and defensive in his private life.

On the other hand, middle children have had to learn to live in peace with the very different personalities of the youngest and oldest of their siblings and, as a result, they may be quite adept at dealing with all kinds of people. As the bridge between siblings, they learn the art of negotiation and compromise early on in order to get what they want. Lech Walesa, a middle child, was first a protester, but then became a force for moderation and mediation between the unions and the Polish Communist government. Some middles may carry peacemaking to the extreme of attempting to please everyone and keep the peace at any price. They may even change loyalties just to keep all the bases covered and everyone happy, and they can appear inconsistent and prone to waffling as a result. George McGovern suffered from this image during his 1972 presidential campaign, but it was because his mission was to be a peacemaker. "The most important issue of our time is the establishment... of world peace," he often said.

Karl Konig, an early writer on birth order, said "The first born attempts to conquer the world. The third born is inclined to escape the direct meeting with the world. The second born tries to live in harmony with the world."

It is not unusual in families for splits and divisions of opinion to take place with, for example, the parents on one side and the kids on the other or the males on one side and the females on the other or mom on one side with one or more children and dad on the other with the rest of the children. One response of a middle child to these opposing camps may be to try to serve as a mediator.

Renee came into therapy because of the stress she was feeling about her 70-year-old parents who were threatening divorce (in fact they had done this for many years, but most recently her mother had moved out for a week). Renee's older brother was on his mother's side and saw his father as an unloving man. Renee's younger sister was on her father's side and believed the story that her mother was an angry alcoholic.

Renee found herself not only trying to mediate the fights between her parents but also between her brother and sister. It was not so much that she could see both sides of the story, but that she felt the need to keep the family together and to keep the peace. The amount of time and energy and worry that went into this was taking its toll on her and her own marriage. Her husband was threatening to leave her if she continued her high level of involvement in this issue, which had actually been a part of their seven years of married life.

Therapy helped Renee to look at her role as peacekeeping middle child and to begin to think about what might happen if she let go of that role. She invited her brother and sister to join her therapy sessions, and the three of them began to look at how they had developed their triangular positions with each other, and what it would mean for each of them to get out of the marital conflicts between mom and dad.

It took them quite a while to sort this through for themselves, but they were eventually able to let go of their side-taking and mediating roles. Their parents continued to try to pull them into fights and get support for their side, but the children, after about six months of work, were able to successfully avoid getting involved, while still maintaining friendly contact with both.

After a year of being able to maintain this new stance, and of Renee not trying to make things peaceful, mom and dad, after 40 years of marital upset and fighting, finally began to settle down and make a modicum of peace with each other.

Middle children are also susceptible to becoming the "lost" sibling. If they have not been successful in carving out an identity within the family, they may withdraw and disappear, emotionally or even physically. They begin to feel alone in the world, uncared for, and unremarkable. Trusting that anybody cares for them or is interested in them becomes difficult.

Janice was the middle girl of a sister nearly four years older and a brother three years younger. She had enjoyed some of the attention of being a youngest for three years but with the birth of her brother she felt "dropped" by her parents. He became the apple of their eye, and she could never compete with the skills and abilities of her sister. She went through a period in her teens of being angry and rebellious, but this didn't change her sense of being "no place and no one" in the family. She thought she was seen by her parents as "just a problem."

When she moved out to live on her own, she began a number of brief relationships with men and was highly promiscuous. She began to drink too much and to abuse a variety of drugs. Most of the men she dated were disrespectful of her emotionally. When she did meet a more considerate and caring man she quickly began to feel uncomfortable with him and refused to trust in or believe that he genuinely liked her. She came in to therapy because she was beginning to think she might act on her frequent suicidal fantasies.

It took her quite a while to begin to have the courage to reconnect in a more meaningful way with her family members. She started with her siblings and explored with them their perceptions of family life and their various roles. Eventually she was able to talk to her mother and father, not to say "why didn't you love me more?" but to find out more about their own experience as children in their families of origin. Janice began to understand the implications of her mother being an oldest (like Janice's sister) and her father being a youngest (like her brother). They had both had middle siblings who were "problems" in the family and had eventually withdrawn from their families.

She saw that her problems were not just hers but were part of a multigenerational pattern. As she continued to show a sincere interest in her parents' early experiences of family, they began to talk more, on their own initiative, about how they had seen their middle siblings mirrored in Janice. The frustrations they had felt in dealing with their siblings had come to the surface again in dealing with her. They both felt terrible about the way it had gone with Janice. They just didn't know how to break the pattern. Eventually Janice began to feel closer to her parents and more a part of the family. Each of the family members valued her interest in them and her efforts to be closer to them; they had feared that she hated them.

There is, of course, a huge variety of middle positions, with endless variations in the ages and sexes and numbers of other siblings — far too many to discuss individually. But generally, middle children get short shrift.

The distribution of the sexes and ages of siblings is of crucial importance to the personality development of the middle child. In general, the middle child will tend to develop birth order characteristics in reaction to the sibling he or she is closest to in age or spent the most time with as a child. In other words, if the middle child is a girl two years younger than the oldest boy and then there is a gap of four years and another girl, she will be more like a youngest sister of brothers than an oldest sister of sisters. But she will have some of the characteristics of the latter position as well.

If the middle child is third after a gap of three years with a younger sibling coming a year later, he or she will be more like an oldest. The middle child who is in the exact center will share more of both youngest and oldest characteristics and will be the most confused of middle children.

Sometimes the middle child who is second may take over the role of the oldest if the oldest abdicates in some way — either from illness or from being so discouraged by the threat to the throne that he or she gives up defending the position. This is especially likely to occur if the first is a girl and the second is a boy and they are close in age. Perhaps because of the fuss made over the first boy or because of the overt or unconscious sexism of the parents, the second child takes on the role of oldest, displacing his older sister, who then develops more like a youngest sister. This was undoubtedly the case with John D. Rockefeller, who was called a "shrewd anaconda" in business and acted like the older brother of a brother, which he was, despite also having an older sister.

This elevation of the middle boy due to sexism was even more common earlier in history. Thomas Jefferson, the middle of eight girls and a youngest boy who was mentally handicapped, naturally assumed the role of oldest, most successful child because he was a boy. Antarctic explorer Robert Falcon Scott was also a middle who was the oldest son in his family.

This kind of reallocation in roles also occurs in reverse for girls. A middle girl who has only older brothers may have to take on much more family responsibility than those older boys do. Although rock star Madonna had two older brothers, she, as the oldest girl, was expected to look after the three younger children following her mother's death.

If all the children are the same sex, the middle child is at the greatest disadvantage. Middle children in this position tend to receive the least attention and affirmation from parents and have the most need to try to stand out in some way. They are often the most anxious and self-critical among the children in a family. They may give up trying to be noticed and just become depressed or they may become hostile and argumentative in order to be noticed.

Pablo, a middle brother of brothers, spoke of how he always fought with his older brother, Carlos, who usually won the fights. When the fight was over, Carlos would go to Manuel, the youngest brother, and do something that was warm, caring, and "brotherly." The two of them would go off together, leaving Pablo alone. Pablo regularly felt left out in the cold. He wasn't as close to either Carlos or Manuel as they were to each other. He was sad and tearful as he recounted this history.

His therapist suggested that there might have been a kind of closeness involved in the fighting between him and Carlos — a negative, but intense, closeness. Pablo needed to find a way to shift it from a negative context to a positive one. When he began to work on this he discovered that being argumentative was still his way of making contact with people and that he didn't know how to do it any differently.

After some time, he began to realize how much of his identity had been shaped in his fights with his oldest brother. When he wasn't opposing people, he was uncertain about how to act and felt ill at ease. Although he had thought of himself as an independent person, he could see how much he needed people to fight with in order to feel like himself. He only felt affirmed when he could get someone to take notice of him, which he thought he could do only by arguing with the person.

Part of Pablo's work on changing this pattern involved identifying his fear of closeness that was caring rather than conflictual. He feared it mostly because he didn't know how to be warm and close. He also felt extremely vulnerable if he didn't, physically or symbolically, "put up his dukes" at every encounter.

He slowly began to restrain his automatic hostile reaction to others and found that he was able to have better relationships as a result. He also began to experience a new kind of warmth and closeness with his oldest brother as he stopped disagreeing with everything Carlos said and started listening more.

The middle girl of girls seems to face even more disadvantages than the middle brother of brothers. She has the misfortune to be the least favored sex in the least favored position. One early study of families found that parents of daughters, without being conscious of it, least preferred their middle daughter. As a result, the middle sister of sisters can turn into a very difficult, excitable, demanding child. She may drop out entirely or try hard to be different from her two sisters. If they are good, she may be bad. She may start stealing or lying to excess. If they are career-oriented, she may excel as a homemaker; if they enjoy being homemakers, she may climb the career ladder.

Joan Baez is the middle of three half-Mexican girls — a brilliant, shy older sister and a beautiful baby sister. As a child, she was different from and, she thought, inferior to them because she was darker in color. Then she discovered that her voice could help her be different in a positive sense.

The more interests the oldest and youngest girls have, the narrower the range of choices for this middle. The feminist writer Kate Millett is a middle sister of sisters who is very aware of the disadvantages of her birth position and very vocal in her anger about the way women in general are treated.

The middle sister of sisters needs special attention and caring from her father, who may have wanted a boy in her place so tends to ignore her while finding her younger sister, the new baby, too cute to resist.

I was a great disappointment because my parents had been hoping for a boy. I was christened Friederike, the name given to every second daughter in my mother's family....My father, unable to reconcile himself to the fact that I was a girl, called me Fritz, treated me as if I were a son, and encouraged me to wear boy's clothes.

Joy Adamson, *The Searching Spirit*

Middle children whose siblings are all of the opposite sex may receive most of the attention in the family, being nurtured by the older siblings and looked up to by the younger ones. These middles may be so pampered all around that marriage is out of the question for them since the situation at home is impossible to duplicate. Middle children in this position often have difficulty making friends with peers of the same sex. Ernest Hemingway, a middle boy with four sisters, found it difficult to stick with one woman as an adult, and he made a career out of trying to be macho and "one of the boys."

A boy who is the middle of two girls needs a lot of contact with his father to maintain his gender identity and learn to be assertive when necessary. He may sometimes assume the role of oldest since he is the oldest son.

The middle child who is a different sex from the first and the same as the last may have the best of it. There is less need to compete with the first child, the parents react favorably to the arrival of a different sex child, and the arrival of a same-sex last child reinforces the gender identity of the middle child.

Life is better for middle children if they come from a larger family with siblings of both sexes. There seems to be less competition and jealousy because the siblings form many different subgroups and factions. Youngest and oldest may form a group while the several middles form their own groupings. Or consecutively aged siblings may form two or three different groups, with some of the middles in the role of youngest and some in the role of oldest.

Walt Disney, with three older brothers and a younger sister, had an antagonistic relationship with his two oldest brothers. But he was close to his next oldest brother, who became a loving father figure for him, a substitute for his actual father who was something of a tyrant.

In some cases, middle children turn out to be the happiest adults since they have lower expectations than other birth orders and an ability to cope with life without being as compulsive as the oldest. They are more relaxed and more considerate than the oldest and more achievement oriented than the youngest. Older middles who are encouraged by their parents may achieve as much as an oldest, but with less stress. Pope John XXIII was an older middle of 12 children, following 3 girls, and proved to be a kind, humanitarian leader of the church, less concerned than other popes with authority and discipline and more willing to try "radical" new things.

A middle who is the second of four may be competitive with the oldest and, like the oldest, try to emulate the parents, but is usually less anxious and tense. For instance, a second oldest girl may be motherly, but not as strict or domineering as her older sister.

The middle who is third of four, say, may be more like a youngest — easygoing and not under any pressure to succeed. Mark Twain, the fifth of six children, was "wild and mischievous, often exasperating, manipulative," according to biographer Albert Bigelow Paine. "A perpetual nuisance," his mother joked. His oldest brother, who described himself as "gloomy, taciturn, and selfish," wrote that the family missed Mark's "abounding activity and merriment" after he moved away. Like many youngests, he was never able to settle down for long and couldn't hang on to his money.

b. AS A SPOUSE

Middles do well in friendship and marriage with most other birth orders. Middles married to middles may have a very calm relationship because they are both willing to negotiate and want to avoid problems. If they do have conflicts, they may avoid them so much that resentments accumulate to the point that it becomes too late to save the situation. They are better off when they can be honest with each other and face the difficulties. They may also both need to work on assuming responsibilities.

Middle children who were made the beloved pet of their opposite-sex siblings may have difficulty getting enough attention in a relationship with just one person of the opposite sex.

Mona started therapy when she was 34 because she was unable to commit herself to a relationship with a man. She always had several men interested in her at any one time. Her pattern was to date one seriously for a year or two, begin to consider marriage, and then panic at the thought of being tied down. At that point, she would begin to find things she didn't like about the man and break off with him, usually to the man's great distress. Then she started over with a new man.

Mona was the middle sister of two brothers. Her experience as a child was that of being doted on by all three men in her family — two brothers and father — and being treated as a special person all her life. She participated in all of their male games and activities, but never had any of the heavy work they had. She had the fun, but not the responsibilities of the males. They took care of her too well. By becoming aware of this dynamic she could see how settling for just one man in her life seemed, subconsciously, like a loss to her and how she sabotaged her relationships to avoid it.

Middle children may stay in destructive relationships longer than most people because they don't want to give up the place they have made for themselves outside the family and are willing to keep trying to make it work.

c. AS A PARENT

Middle children usually enjoy being parents and do it well. They are comfortable with having more people in the household since they came from a family of at least three children.

Their specific patterns of parenting depend on their positioning within the middle grouping — whether they are more like oldests or more like youngests. Usually, however, they accept the responsibilities of parenthood more easily than youngests and are more relaxed than oldests.

d. AS A FRIEND

Middle children who feel overlooked at home may seek out their peers for affirmation, and they are often the most social of the children. They are usually very friendly to everyone and look for friendships outside the family. With their friends they feel separate and unique and accepted as equals. They are usually well liked by other children and can be popular as adults.

He was not first in his class nor brilliant in his studies....He was a nice fellow, yes, liked by everybody, but not much noticed among the rest. He was above all a dreamer.

Curtis Cate, writing about middle child Antoine de Saint-Exupery, in *Antoine de Saint-Exupery: His Life and Times*

Middles, with their experience of living with both youngests and oldests, can be good friends to people in most birth positions. Middles who have both-sex siblings are usually well rounded and make friends easily. Their best same-sex friendships usually duplicate their position in the family. A middle girl with older brother and younger sister is likely to get along best with a youngest sister of sisters.

Middles who are the opposite sex of all their siblings will have the most trouble making same-sex friends and may end up seeking intimacy only in love relationships.

e. AT WORK

By trying to live in harmony with the world, including older and younger siblings and parents, middle children usually become skilled at handling people and make good career diplomats, mediators, secretaries, barbers, and waiters — positions that require tact and patience, but not much aggressiveness.

They can also be good middle managers since they understand the needs of people and deal well with the ups and downs of relationships, but they may lack the ability to supervise tasks well. Because many of them crave attention and affection, they also go into the entertainment field. Dolly Parton, for example, is the fourth of twelve children.

They are less likely than oldests or youngests to become famous or eminent in their field. However, as noted above, many middle sons move into the role of high achieving oldest if they have only older sisters or their older brother abdicates in some way.

Middle child Donald Trump had an older brother who was named after their father and who was supposed to follow in his footsteps, but didn't measure up. Donald, younger and more rebellious, competed with this brother for his father's attention and won his father's respect by standing up to him. The older brother died as a middle-aged alcoholic, while Donald went on to score his reputedly ruthless business triumphs.

Michelangelo, the second of five brothers, was in line to fill the role of oldest when his older brother decided to go into the church. He did take on the role of the oldest by becoming pre-eminent in his field; however, to the dismay of his father, he chose art rather than the family business.

f. TO THE PARENTS OF A MIDDLE CHILD

Treat your middle child with care and respect. Don't make assumptions that everything is fine just because you don't hear any complaints. Give your middle child responsibilities, solicit opinions, ask about feelings. In other words, pay more attention to your middle child and make him or her feel special. And take a lot of photos.

g. TO THE ADULT MIDDLE CHILD

You would do well to stop comparing yourself to your siblings and instead think of yourself the way those outside your family do: as a unique individual with the advantage of being able to get along well with almost everybody. You might also think about what you want for yourself and risk some confrontations occasionally to get it rather than ignoring your wants all the time.

11
ONE OF A KIND: ONLY CHILDREN IN GENERAL

Being an only child is a disease in itself.

Psychologist G. Stanley Hall, circa 1885

a. GENERAL CHARACTERISTICS

Only children have suffered from a bad image in the past, but recent research indicates that they are usually as well adjusted as people with brothers and sisters — if not better. An only child goes around "disguised as a normal person," as comedian David Steinberg would say.

This is good news, since there are likely to be more only children in the world in the 21st century as governments in the east try to limit population growth and parents in the west struggle to combine two careers with parenting. Even today, 20% of American mothers who say they have finished their families have only one child, double the number of only-child families just 10 years ago.

Children who have no siblings have the best and worst of all possible worlds: they are perpetually the over-achieving oldest and the pampered youngest in the family. As a result, they have many of the characteristics of an oldest child, yet may remain childlike in many ways into adulthood. Many only children look much younger than they are even when quite old.

Since only children are never displaced by younger siblings, they are never in the position of having to defend their position as the favored child of their parents. They are more often considered special and precious by their parents than children who have siblings. Because they never have to share their parents, they know their position in the family is assured no matter what. They have less resentment of authority than youngests and actually expect, as well as accept, help from others when they need it. Because they don't have to compete for attention with any younger intruders, they tend to be more at ease with themselves and have a higher self-esteem than oldest children, with less need to control others.

If they don't get the attention they want from one person, they are not likely to fight for it, but will just move on to someone else.

I was one of the lucky only children; my sense of self-importance and ability to amuse myself paid off.

John Updike, *Self-Consciousness*

More than other children, the only child picks up the characteristics of the same-sex parent's sibling position. For example, a female only child whose mother is the youngest sister of sisters may be more flighty and flirtatious than one whose mother is the oldest sister of brothers.

In fact, the only child may be very much like the same-sex parent until faced with some difficulty or stress, at which time the only-child characteristics will show up. At the same time, only children have their opposite-sex parent to themselves and may identify more strongly with that parent than children with siblings do. And without siblings to reinforce their sex role, onlies are often more androgynous than other children.

Only children tend to compete with their same-sex parent for the attention and affection of their opposite-sex parent — and they often win, especially if there are problems between the couple. Some researchers claim that incestuous behavior is more widespread in only-child families. When a male only child spends more time with his mother than his father does, mother and son may become the couple in the family. The boy may stay close and dependent on mother throughout his life.

Parents may strictly discipline an only child in their efforts to make the child a worthy representative of their parenting abilities. They have only one chance to do the job right, so they expect the child to be "perfect." As a result, only children often mature early and miss out on being playful or silly. They can become overachievers or may give up completely when they see they can't possibly be perfect.

Without other children to worry about, the parents have more attention to give to the only. That child may become the focus of their lives, receiving a concentrated dose of whatever the parents have to give: love, criticism, anger, joy, fear. If the parents happen to be angry, violent people, it is very traumatic for an only child as the sole recipient of those reactions. If the parents have any emotional problems, an only child has to face them without the support and reality testing that siblings would provide. If, on the other hand, the parents are emotionally comfortable themselves, the only child can be the most secure and contented of the birth orders.

It may be true that an only child is spoiled, not so much with gifts as with the time allotted to his problems, but believe me there are occasions on which he wishes there was a brother or a sister to share the brunt....he tends to become self-centered....he spends more time alone, and in the company of adults.

Peter Ustinov, *Dear Me*

Some only children seek relief from all this adult attention. They may withdraw and become overly independent. They may try to do things quickly before the parents can offer advice, or try to do something so well the first time that no help is needed. The perfectionism of some only children serves as a way to avoid adult interference rather than as a source of self-satisfaction.

Onlies usually resent criticism and will avoid doing something a second time if they have been criticized for the way they did it the first time. They saw their parents apparently doing things perfectly and they seldom saw other children trying a new thing over and over before getting it right.

Parents of onlies may not be very accepting of a child's need to play and be messy. They often hover over the child, picking up toys and talking about tasks to be done. This can lead onlies to find it difficult in later life to separate work from play. They may not truly enjoy the play and not completely settle down to work.

Children tend to live in their own world, with their own sense of what is important, and adults cannot share in this. Adults just don't have the same responses to things. Only children miss out on having someone at their own level to talk to about what they consider important. If they have ever been laughed at for being "childish," they may always be guarded about showing their feelings or saying what they think.

Only children generally expect a lot from life. After all, they have had a lot while growing up, both psychologically and materially. Even in families that are not well off, the only child is the sole beneficiary of whatever resources are available. The only child not only has more or better toys, but as an adult doesn't have to share any inheritance. This doesn't mean that only children are necessarily spoiled or greedy — they are often as frugal and careful with money as with their other possessions. Nor are they very acquisitive. Their needs have already been more than adequately met. Only child Ingrid Bergman wrote about asking her father for her weekly pocket money of one krona and being given instead a handful of kronas. She would say, "You mustn't do that, you mustn't spoil me. I should just have one krona a week." But he would insist, and she'd take two to please him.

Since parents of onlies tend to have the same high expectations as parents of oldest children, onlies usually excel at school. If they have been smothered by attention at home, school may be a welcome relief. They may also enjoy it as a place where they can shine in relation to others, unlike at home. They are likely to become "teacher's pet" not just because they are good, quiet students but because they may feel more comfortable with the teacher than with the other children.

Only children, especially males, tend to be high achievers: Franklin Delano Roosevelt, Walter Cronkite, John Kenneth Galbraith, H.R. MacMillan, and Ansel Adams are examples. They may get very upset if they do not succeed at everything they do. They are, in fact, usually successful; in most tests of scholastic ability they are the highest scorers of all birth positions. In one series of studies on intelligence, however, only children and oldest children had the same scores. Researchers had expected only children to do best since all other cases showed a correlation between high scores and fewer siblings. The researchers came to the conclusion that only children did less well than expected because they had no younger siblings to teach. Since teaching reinforces learning, the oldest children scored higher.

No matter how successful only children are, they may continue to fear failure and dread letting down their parents. Unlike oldest children who internalize their need to achieve and do it out of self-need, only children more often work to please others.

Having had only themselves to depend on for play, only children are often quite adept at using their imagination in fantasy play and finding ways to entertain themselves. They are the most likely children to create imaginary friends, which are easier to cope with than real friends. One 12-year-old only child, who was particularly envious of her friends' siblings, fantasized about having a family of 17 brothers and sisters, with herself a twin and the two of them exactly in the middle of all the others. However, when it came time for her to have children as an adult, she decided she'd rather not have any. She didn't want to be the caretaker herself.

Having had fewer opportunities for real play with other children, onlies tend to be less playful than others, and when young may act like miniature adults, often to the delight of parents and other adults who think they are being cute as well as "good." However, this means that the only child may not know childhood games and may have no opportunity to do such things as practice dancing with siblings as a pre-teen or try out jokes. The parents of only children are most often older than the norm and therefore less playful themselves.

Until I was 11...I thought I was a small adult.

W.P. Kinsella, "Kinsella writes what pleases him"

Only children may excel at adult things and have a wide range of interests, but not be good at child things and feel out of place with other children. They are, for instance, likely to get a two-wheel bike later than other children. Experiences like this may make them feel slightly handicapped in social situations later on. On the other hand, years of sitting quietly in adult company make them good observers of the human condition, and they are often able to figure out all the sides of an argument.

Because their first conversations were with adults, only children usually have highly developed verbal skills, but as adults they often end up being the least talkative. They have no experience with the easy give and take of social bantering among peers. A few may become extreme loners or eccentrics, but most do learn to relate well to others and become socially well-adjusted.

We assume that only children are spoiled and pampered; but they also are made to share adult perspectives. Possibly the household that nurtured me was a distracted and needy

one...which asked me to grow up too early....If I'm nice and good, you'll leave me alone to read my comic books. Have I ever loved a human being as purely as I loved Mickey Mouse or, a bit later in latency, Captain Marvel and Plastic Man?

John Updike, *Self-Consciousness*

In all families, grown children are more important to their parents than their parents are to them, but in only-child families this is intensified. Only children often have difficulty breaking away from home. They can't leave their parents, especially a single parent, without feeling guilty and disloyal. They may feel particularly burdened in later life when their elderly parents need care. They are the least capable in many ways of taking good care of their parents, yet there is no one else who can assume this responsibility. They, particularly males, may end up ignoring problems or being only sporadically helpful.

For only children who were born in the 1960s or earlier, there is one other significant factor to consider: why are they only children? Before the lifestyle changes of the 1970s and later, when many working couples began to decide they could manage only one child, it was extremely unusual for parents to have just one child. The older single child often signals some trouble with the parents — physical, emotional, or financial — that prevented them from having other children. If there were problems in the home, these would also have a significant impact on the only child's personality development. For example, many only children are onlies because their parents divorced. Such additional complications have to be taken into consideration in any discussion of only children.

Only child Joseph worked even harder at being "good" after his parents divorced when he was four. He thought he had already lost one parent, and he did not want to lose another by misbehaving. This made him even more cautious, eager to please adults, and overly mature for his age. He was a proper gentleman at age six, but isolated from playmates and without joy in his life. He brought this stance into his marriage and it was difficult for him to interact spontaneously and playfully with his wife.

Difficulties with pregnancy and labor were another reason for only-child families before 1960, and this too affected the child's development. When the only child has come after repeated attempts to have children, or after a miscarriage or death, the parents are more likely than ever to spoil and over-protect the child, creating a self-centered adult. These parents may be overly concerned about the physical health of their only child and over-react to normal childhood illnesses, creating an adult who pays too much attention to minor physical ailments and expects others to be equally upset about these problems.

Parents who have simply made a lifestyle decision to have one child are usually older, better educated, more liberal, and more successful in their careers. However, their world is also likely to be highly structured and their child may be expected to fit neatly into it without too much disruption or rocking of the boat. In the past, parents of a male first-born have been more likely to stop at one child voluntarily than parents of a first-born female, so there have been more male onlies than female onlies. Whether this will change as attitudes toward gender change is an open question.

Alfred Adler, in the beginning of the 20th century, spoke of only children as growing up in a pessimistic family. At the beginning of the 21st century it is more likely that the only child is growing up in a happy, well-off, two-career family.

b. AS A SPOUSE

Since only children are not used to living intimately with other children, they often don't know how to cope with intimate relationships later in life. They may have difficulty accepting or understanding normal mood changes and inconsistencies in others. They like to be organized, tidy, and punctual, and have trouble with people — especially spouses — who are not.

They are used to their own well-defined structure, and don't like to be taken by surprise. If they have made plans to do something, it is hard for them to change spontaneously or to be flexible.

They haven't learned the fine art of negotiation and don't understand the necessity of sharing control or anything else. They simply haven't been called upon to share anything — their room, their clothes, their toys, their books are all theirs. While they may be willing to share things as adults, it's usually only on condition that everything is "put back in its proper place in good condition."

The very way he spoke of his brother and sister...came from a kind of human experience I would never know.... Without wanting a brother or sister for myself — Where would they sleep? What would they eat? Who would prevent them from using my toys and pencils and crayons? I enjoyed this aspect of my father.

John Updike, *Self-Consciousness*

Since parents don't often admit their mistakes or say to a child that they were wrong and are sorry, only children also do not learn the art of apologizing. They find it just as difficult to forgive others as to forgive themselves. If they've been over-indulged or unrealistically praised, they develop a false sense of their own abilities and powers. Even the mildest rebuke can be deeply wounding, much to the surprise of a spouse who may be accustomed to trading mild insults with siblings with no repercussions.

Onlies are used to things going smoothly for them. They haven't had to deal with interruptions or harassment from siblings, so when something does go wrong their reactions may be quite out of proportion to the importance of the event. What others see as a minor problem, the only may see as a disaster. Even something like a small disagreement can be taken as a personal affront.

Because they prefer to focus on just one relationship at a time, most only children are quite comfortable with monogamy; they are even more comfortable with living alone. Marriage to anyone of any birth order can be a challenge for them.

c. AS A PARENT

Only children generally have more difficulty with being parents than people in other birth orders. In addition to not having any experience in dealing with younger children in the family, they are unaccustomed to having many other people around.

Onlies are the most likely adults to not have children or to have just one child. Some onlies, however, want to make up for their own lonely childhood by having several children of their own. They realize too late that being a child in a large family is a lot easier than being a parent of a large family.

When onlies do have children, they tend to fob off most of the responsibility for them on their spouse. This can work well if the spouse is an oldest, but creates problems if the spouse is a youngest or, worse, another only.

d. AS A FRIEND

Onlies tend to want just one close friend at a time. They may cling to one person to prevent loneliness, yet still be most comfortable alone. They usually prefer individual sports, such as swimming, over team sports. They have trouble adjusting to the different personalities of too many peers at the same time. Some are fearful about meeting new people and have to force themselves into social situations.

As children, onlies who visit homes where there are many siblings are often amazed to see how a family with so many people lives. The only child can seem like a being from Mars observing what, for other people, are everyday happenings. Peter Ustinov reports that his own children taught him much about "the human condition, relatively obvious things that had just never occurred" to him.

I early developed a pronounced allergy to any sort of organized sport which has been with me ever since. Perhaps it's because I was an only child, but I have never felt any sort of team spirit.

At the beginning, when I was away at school, I was extremely lonely. Loneliness, however, the birthright of the only child, held no particular terrors for me.

John Mortimer, *Clinging to the Wreckage: A Part of Life*

When social situations become stressful, only children may revert to their loner selves. They have no experience with having to deal with peers — especially someone they find upsetting — on an ongoing basis. They have never learned about "forgiving and forgetting" and don't always realize that the person who is angry with them now may soon be laughing and joking again.

They take slights more personally than others, too. A friend who has other friends can seem disloyal to an only child — after all, the only child is content with one friend at a time. It's no accident that the author of the line "Hell is — other people" was an only child: Jean-Paul Sartre.

This is not to say that only children don't like other people and even, perhaps, long to be part of a group. But only children just aren't used to dealing with the complexities of other human beings.

I was a lonely child, though I was not conscious of loneliness; in fact, I preferred to be on my own. At the same time, I was torn by the desire to be with other people, to be part of a circle...yet after being together with my cousins for a while, I longed to be alone.

James Kirkup, *The Only Child: An Autobiography of Infancy*

e. AT WORK

Only children are often eager to please older people or those in authority, but they have also learned early on how to manipulate them. Some onlies take advantage of their special position in their family by making slaves of their parents and go on to become domineering as adults. These only children may need constant affirmation and reassurance as a continuation of the early adult approval. They are shocked when the world does not automatically provide this affirmation.

Often, only children learn to stall, knowing that eventually the parents will help or do the task entirely. As a result, most adult onlies are not self-starters. They usually need a jump start, though once they get going they do excellent work.

When they are little, only children measure their achievements against their parents'. In order to meet parental standards, they keep trying harder to do it better. In later life, they continue to try to please parents and parent-figures — teachers, bosses — so they become conscientious and reliable. Therefore, they have little patience with people who don't meet deadlines or follow through on their commitments.

If something can't be made perfect, an only child may prefer to give it up entirely rather than settle for less. Moderation is not good enough: it has to be all or nothing. Note the every-blade-of-grass-perfect photographs of Ansel Adams, for example. One only child whose productivity at work was low because he insisted that every piece of work be perfect was finally convinced by his boss to give up striving for perfection and settle for excellence instead.

f. TO THE PARENTS OF AN ONLY CHILD

Remember that standards of behavior are different for children than for adults and perhaps your expectations should be lower. Treat your child as a child and encourage playfulness, silliness, and risk taking. Let your child know that it's okay to make mistakes and not be perfect.

Limit your praise to what your child has actually done well; too much praise for minor accomplishments gives a child a false sense of his or her abilities and of what the world's reactions will be.

Don't overindulge your child just because you are able to. Try to dispense the same amount of your time, money, and attention to your only child that you would if you were splitting it up among two or more children.

Be aware that evenings and summer vacations can seem like long, lonely times for a child with no siblings. It may be helpful to let your child invite friends to go on vacation with your family and come over often to play and spend the night. Pets are often especially important to only children and can be one way the child learns how to take care of others.

12
THE MALE ONLY CHILD

He that hath one hog makes him fat;
And he that hath one son makes him a fool.

Proverb

a. GENERAL CHARACTERISTICS

In keeping with the findings about the preference of most parents for having at least one boy, male only children are more favored in their families than female only children. The male only is the favorite of two adults and, in most families, accustomed to having their continual approval, encouragement, and sympathy. And he thinks the rest of the world should treat him with the same acclaim. When the acclaim comes, however, he tends to take it for granted.

...[there] sits a two-year-old child with curly blond hair, beautiful, adored, Poulou, the child-king.

Annie Cohen-Solal, writing about only child
Jean-Paul Sartre in *Sartre: A Life*

The death of his mother is the greatest loss for the male only. His mother is the one who thinks he can do anything, which he usually can. But to do so, he may need the background support of his mother or a substitute mother figure all his life.

A male only child runs the risk of becoming a mama's boy, unless his mother has other strong interests. This is particularly true when the parents are separated and he is expected to be "her man."

Noah's father died when he was one year old, and his young, attractive mother had to go back to work to support the two of them. As a therapist later explained to him, Noah was extremely lucky that his mother was a youngest sister of brothers and had less commitment to parenting than to her social life. She dated often, married and divorced twice, and through it all adored her son, but left him pretty much on his own. He developed the standard characteristics of an only, with more emphasis on the loner side and less on the spoiled side. His only real handicap in life was his rabid self-sufficiency. If she had been more focused on him emotionally, he would not have had the freedom to move out into the world as easily and as confidently as he did.

Having not been trained to "be nice to brother...," the male only can't be expected to offer much support to others. He usually won't go out of his way for anybody, unless he's just as happy to go that way as another anyway. But it isn't for that reason that the male only child is often a loner. He may be charming and others may be attracted to him, but he just doesn't pursue friendships very vigorously. Only child and loner Farley Mowat writes, "it is only in the [Canadian] north that I find people I admire."

The male only often finds sharing difficult. Even as a 40-year-old, Teddy didn't want to share his favorite things. His wife was amazed one day when Teddy's best friend dropped in for a visit, and Teddy stopped her from offering some freshly baked chocolate chip cookies to his friend. The cookies were for Teddy, and he didn't want to part with any of them.

The male only has a basic sense of security about himself and doesn't usually worry about financial security. At some level of his consciousness, he expects that he will always be taken care of and that he will always be liked no matter what he does.

I was the only child, and was extremely spoiled, but I continually heard from my mother how very much happier I was than she had been....

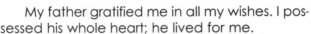

My father gratified me in all my wishes. I possessed his whole heart; he lived for me.

Hans Christian Andersen,
The Fairy Tale of My Life

In a group, the male only can remain neutral and objective, because he's not competing for what he thinks is already his by right. Since he has always been the center of attention, he may expect to be in that position without having to do anything to earn it. If it turns out that he isn't being paid attention to as an adult, he may just depart from the scene.

Len was a friendly, easy-going only child, but he did not want to go to parties or be in social groups unless he was in an "authorized" position of some kind as leader. Then he enjoyed the social contacts and the other people. When not in this role, he just quietly withdrew and would not make an effort to "get the floor" by himself. In therapy he had to consciously work at learning how to participate in the give and take of social groups. Even though he learned how to do this, he never lost the sense of relief he felt when he went home.

Some male onlies go to the extreme edge of being a loner, such as child prodigy pianist Glen Gould.

b. AS A SPOUSE

For a mate, the male only child can take or leave just about any woman. His is the birth order most likely to remain single. He really isn't well suited to any peer relationship; he's used to having his parents take care of his basic needs while letting him do what he wants. So the wife of a male only child is expected to make life easier for him without asking for much in return. And she has to adjust to his lifestyle since he is rarely flexible enough to adjust to hers. If he has always been served dinner at 6:00 p.m., for example, he will want dinner at 6:00 p.m., not 6:15 p.m.

He is not likely to share his feelings with his wife. He keeps a stiff upper lip no matter what.

Since he would be an oldest brother if there had been other children in his family, he is sometimes well matched with a younger or middle sister of brothers, although life with a youngest may seem too chaotic to him with his need for order. The oldest or middle sister of brothers can do well at being a mother for him, and he may respect and admire her, although they usually aren't very close.

Another only child is usually the most difficult mate for an only child. Despite what they have in common, both of them have trouble dealing with the stress and strain of a close peer relationship, neither of them is used to the opposite sex, both are used to having their own way, and both want the other to play nurturing parent.

On the other hand, if they are both involved in careers and have few external problems to cope with, two onlies can live well together like "two solitudes" because they each respect the other's need for privacy and autonomy. They may be the most content of all people with monogamy as they don't particularly want the company of other people and can only handle one intimate relationship at a time. When only children do marry each other, they often decide (wisely) not to have children.

In the past, when almost everyone got married, male onlies married at a younger age than other men, but also divorced more. Some male onlies are not comfortable having sex with their wife who may be too much like a mother figure for them; they prefer to have sex with women they don't know well.

c. AS A PARENT

If the male only child has children, his wife usually has to take the sole responsibility for them, especially when they are younger. He rarely wants to be involved with the parenting. He can enjoy being involved with them as long as they are not too demanding or problematic, and are willing to go along with what he wants. Failing this, he will leave them with their mother.

He also may miss being the focus of attention in the family and not be comfortable with the "crowd" of people in the house. He is likely to want to escape from the house as much as possible. He is usually impatient with the noise and clutter of children, and any restrictions he imposes will be to keep them from inconveniencing him rather than to keep them safe or "good." He is unlikely to put much pressure for achievement on his children, but rather will leave them to their own devices. He can be a benign, if slightly indifferent, parent.

d. AS A FRIEND

Male friends are not that important to the male only, but he often attaches himself to an older mentor who appreciates him. He can be an easy, enjoyable companion, though, since he does not feel the need to be competitive and can be so detached that he appears very accepting and undemanding of others. Friends most often criticize him for being stubborn.

More than the female only, he tends to get rattled being with too many other people. The ideal group size for him may be two people, three if necessary, and four at the absolute maximum. The idea of having a party, even to celebrate a milestone like his sixtieth birthday, can be horrifying. He is more likely to have just his wife as a close friend.

He may be friends with an oldest brother of brothers who is also older in age, but is most likely to feel comfortable with other male only children, one at a time.

[At age 12] his narcissism was rudely tested... [he] was suddenly rocked from the Schweitzer paradise — where nothing was too good for the cherished child — to the real world of cruel and violent teenagers who felt only contempt for this pompous little monster with his stuffy speeches, stale wit, absurd appearance, and Parisian manners.

For this outsider, this only child, the outstanding feature of those years was his friendship with another only child....

Annie Cohen-Solal, *Sartre: A Life*

e. AT WORK

The male only child, like the oldest, is often a high achiever, though he usually tries hard in order to please authority figures rather than for his own satisfaction. In general, the male only expects his work situation to be set up so that it shows off his achievements, much like his parents' home did, and he isn't quite happy with his work if those around him aren't often applauding him. He will often risk appearing foolish for the sake of being the center of attention.

Since he doesn't feel the need to compete with co-workers, he is usually good to work with, and he tends to work well under authority, perceiving it as benevolent. He usually has little interest in being involved in office politics and will walk away when a staff group gathers to complain about work. He tends to work more for the sake of the income, which he then wants to enjoy, than for the sake of accomplishing some great goal. While he might dream of gaining glory and recognition, he may be uncomfortable when it comes and not know how to handle it.

A male only would seem to be a prime candidate for political office, but as one commentator has said, he is usually too self-centered to seek high office. He would rather not have to "serve the people," and he values his privacy too greatly to be in the public eye for long. He also finds it difficult to compromise and often can see only one way of doing things — his. Franklin D. Roosevelt was one only child who did make the sacrifices necessary to go into politics. And the two youngest men to serve as state governors in the United States were also only children.

Male onlies are more often scientists, writers, lawyers, artists, scholars, and technicians. If they go into a field like therapy or teaching, they are usually more interested in theories and philosophies than in helping others.

f. TO THE PARENTS OF A MALE ONLY CHILD

In addition to the general advice for only children in chapter 11, make sure your male only child is given plenty of household responsibilities as a child. Don't pamper him. Fathers need to model for the male only how to be with women and how to be nurturing to children.

Mothers should keep in mind that their relationship with their spouse is the most important one. Don't let a son take the role of a surrogate spouse. As well as not being good for the marriage, it is definitely not good for the son, even if he enjoys the special position of confidant or partner. This is a particular danger for single moms who might be tempted to seek emotional support from their child rather than from their peers.

g. TO THE ADULT MALE ONLY CHILD

In general, you would do well to be less demanding of the world around you. Lower your expectations for yourself and others, be less concerned about disorder, be more appreciative of other people, learn to compromise, and be more playful. Try being less in control and allow yourself to be more vulnerable.

Having been a recipient all during childhood, you may need to work at giving to others to experience the pleasure that provides.

Make sure you schedule in enough time to be alone, and since you usually get along best with much older or much younger people, look for friends outside of your own age group.

13
THE FEMALE ONLY CHILD

I am all the daughters of my father's house,
and all the brothers too.

Shakespeare, *Twelfth Night*

a. GENERAL CHARACTERISTICS

The female only child leads a somewhat less blissful life than the male only child, but she still has an underlying sense of herself as a special person — Her Highness — and she is often hurt if others don't treat her that way. She may crave approval, if not adoration, especially from the men in her life. Only child Queen Victoria adored her husband Albert and was completely dependent on him emotionally. She was devastated when he died young, and mourned his loss for 40 years.

If the female only is born following the death of a first child, especially a baby boy, she may have the burden of trying to fill that hole of grief in her parents' lives and never quite measuring up.

She is at once mature for her years and yet perpetually childish. She can go from the extreme of having an intelligent, sophisticated discussion of philosophy or politics one minute to pouting or having a tantrum the next minute if she has not gotten her way in some trivial matter.

She may or may not have been spoiled with material possessions as a child, but usually belongings are not important to her per se. She may have been given gifts much grander than anything she wanted or expected. She is more likely than a male only to feel guilty or embarrassed about being the recipient of such largess in comparison to others, and she more often turns out to be generous and altruistic as an adult, or at least hopes she is thought of that way. However, if she does want something — even a cheap trinket — and doesn't get it, she will be greatly disappointed.

The female only child's parents are usually more protective than the male only's parents and that may lead her to expect similar protection from friends and spouse as an adult. When they live up to these expectations by solving her problems for her, they also inadvertently limit her confidence in her own considerable abilities.

If she was treated too much like a glass doll, she may be helpless and dependent all her life. Usually, however, she is independent and self-sufficient, with a quiet self-confidence. When seven-year-old Marla came home from school with a big lump on her head, she told her mother that a boy in her class had banged her head against the brick wall. Her mother was horrified and rushed up to the school to complain to the principal. She was told that the incident arose because there were two little gangs in the class who were fighting. Marla's mother was outraged that there were gangs in this respectable middle class suburban school. Then the principal said, "Mrs. Jenkins, Marla is the leader of one of the gangs." This gave Marla's mother a new perspective on her daughter.

Janet grew up like an only child, thrown entirely with her parents and their literary friends, who made much of her. It was a strange childhood, but it had the result of giving Janet self-reliance and an independent spirit....a sketch of her at the age of five...shows her already self-possessed and determined.

Lina Waterfield,
writing about her aunt in *Castle in Italy*

Not surprisingly, the female only child tends to be a proponent of women's rights as an adult and to have strong opinions about a number of issues. However, she may not personally achieve as much as her potential would indicate; she often lacks the drive necessary to live up to her potential.

If the female only has been greatly influenced by her mother's sibling position, that will have a moderating effect on the above characteristics. However, she is most likely to identify strongly with and emulate a mother who is an oldest or an only. She has more trouble identifying with the playfulness and fun-loving attitudes of a youngest. She may be more serious and hardworking than her youngest-sister mother.

Her isolation as an only child was relieved somewhat by her studies, but her first 16 years were virtually cloistered. She did not lack security, yet dwelling in fairly untrodden ways had made her introspective....Self-centered, she yearned to express herself. She specialized in being misunderstood.

She was restless and tried to achieve independence....Talented, observant, imaginative, keen-minded, studious....She was neither skilled nor interested in games.

Ralph E. Hove, *Dorothy L. Sayers:*
A Literary Biography

b. AS A SPOUSE

Although independent in lifestyle, a female only is often, in some way, dependent emotionally on a man. However, the man she chooses (and she usually does the choosing, not him) has to be a flexible, easy-going, good-natured man who is able to cope with her willfulness in order for the relationship to work. Only child Wallis Simpson certainly did the choosing when she went after Edward VIII, who gave up his crown to marry her.

A much older man is usually best — someone who is amused rather than threatened by her capriciousness and her tendency to test his love. Since she can't accept criticism easily, she prefers someone who sees only her good points.

She gets divorced less than other women, probably because maintaining the security of marriage is important to her in her sense of aloneness in the world. However, she doesn't take well to household responsibilities and doesn't usually enjoy being a hostess.

Like the male only, the female only can be matched with all male birth positions, but is not well suited for any particular one. She usually has firm ideas about what she wants from a relationship and she expects a lot from a mate. The best choice is usually an oldest brother of sisters. She is likely to let him dominate as long as he takes good care of her needs. Since oldest brothers are the least likely birth order to want a divorce, they are willing to put up with the only female longer than most and will like her independent spirit and charm. If she marries the oldest brother of brothers she often resents the attention he pays to his work.

A middle brother with younger sisters is often a good husband for her. She lets him dominate and he is used to females, but she may expect more career success from him than he is interested in striving for. He may also be too much like an oldest and too career-oriented. A middle brother with several older siblings may have too low self-esteem to win the respect of the female only, but he will try harder than most to stay married.

Since she would have been an oldest if there had been other siblings, the female only sometimes does well with the youngest brother of sisters. They are unlikely to have much of a power struggle and he may be charming to women. However, neither of them will be good at assuming household responsibility or caring for children.

Another only child is the most difficult match as it is unlikely that he will worship her sufficiently or that she will cater to his needs sufficiently. Neither will dominate, and they both tend to be self-indulgent. They have a better chance of making it if they have strong professional or recreational interests in common. But he usually has more need to achieve than she does; her greatest need is for security. They are the least likely of all couples to choose to have children. If they do, they (or the children) often regret it. Her husband may drift away from the home into other pursuits, which threatens her need for a companion and leads to tension in the house for the children. If they both take part in the parenting, they are likely to do it separately, each in their own way, rather than as a team effort. This can lead to confusing contradictions and inconsistencies for their child.

c. AS A PARENT

A female only may not care much about having children regardless of whom she marries, but if she does have children she can be an efficient mother and content to stop working and stay at home.

She is usually less tolerant than other mothers of the noise and mess of children and needs a lot of free time to be alone and quiet. She expects her husband to do a large share of the parenting, which works best if he is an oldest child or a middle with younger brothers and sisters. If she did not enjoy being an only child herself, she will be adamant about having more than one child, even if she feels burdened by it.

She usually does better with boys; if she has a girl she may compete with the child for her husband's attention. She may be even more overprotective and stricter with her children than her parents were, since she never had the opportunity to see them parenting in a more relaxed style with younger siblings. She is likely to try hard to be fair to each child and will treat each one as an only, without giving special privileges to the oldest or special dispensations to the youngest.

d. AS A FRIEND

Female friends of the only are likely to be oldest or middle sisters of sisters or, perhaps, youngest sisters of sisters. Again, the female only is suited to any and to none. However, she, more than the male only, wants to have friends and depends on them for parenting her, even though she appears independent in the relationship.

She may often seek intimacy without having the skills to attain it easily. Bette Midler, playing an only child in the movie *Beaches*, talks on and on about herself and then says to her friend, "That's enough about me. Now, what do you think about me?" The female only often gravitates to older women as friends and is less likely to be a mentor to younger women.

Since she was often alone as a child, she has difficulty understanding others unless they are a lot like her. She often loses patience with people of other birth orders, particularly youngests, who seem too undisciplined to her.

She was old beyond her years because she never had the companionship of other children...

Ellen had to depend upon herself. Books became her friends then, and music....

Daphne Du Maurier, writing about her great-grandmother in *The Du Mauriers*

Merilee, remembering her childhood as an only in an alcoholic home, cried about having had only her books to comfort her. "It's so sad," she said, "they were my only friends and the only things I thought I could trust."

The female only is not usually competitive or envious; she seldom makes comparisons and doesn't care if others have more than she does or do better than she does. Someone else's gain is not her loss — she can even be happy for them. But no one had better try to take away anything of hers that she values — like her man. Only she is allowed to make demands on him.

The loss of parents or parent substitutes is the hardest one for the female only, though her first concern is not for them but for how she will get along without them. She often seeks therapy, but may be disappointed that the therapist doesn't do a better job of taking care of her.

e. AT WORK

A female only is usually quite intelligent and competent, but her talents may be wasted at work unless she has the ideal situation. For her, the ideal situation is a congenial environment where she can work alone or for a kind older man who encourages her often. Then she will outdo herself and more than live up to her potential. Indira Gandhi may have achieved her stature as a world leader because of the encouragement and grooming of her father, Nehru.

Without that kind of sponsorship, the female only usually avoids working very hard and may annoy the people she works with, who will consider her a poor team worker and not of much use. She becomes impatient with committee work and would just as soon "do it myself."

Her lack of goals may make her career path erratic and aimless. She does better when she is the only female working with men. She is more likely to feel threatened by other women than by men. She usually neither understands nor has patience with office politics and holds herself aloof.

She is usually best in independent work and may be a librarian, writer, historian, or designer, or work with elderly people. She often has good ideas, but because she is less talkative than most she keeps them to herself. Only children often end up working in publishing in some way since books may have been their best friends while growing up.

If she goes into fields such as teaching or therapy, she often struggles with it. She usually does best with female students or clients.

f. TO THE PARENTS OF A FEMALE ONLY CHILD

Beware of being overindulgent or overprotective with your female only child. Your daughter will be handicapped in later life if she doesn't experience the usual scrapes and obstacles of childhood and learn how to handle them. She needs boundaries for her behavior but also the freedom to explore and to test her own strengths.

Don't think of your only daughter as a mirror of yourselves. Let her be as different from you as her natural inclinations make her, and allow her to be childish when young. If you are not naturally playful yourselves, make sure she is exposed to plenty of children who are. Encourage her to spend time with friends as much as possible, particularly in their homes with their siblings around.

g. TO THE ADULT FEMALE ONLY CHILD

You may have to work at both being more sociable and not feeling guilty about your need to be alone. Make sure your husband and children or friends know that your desire to be alone does not reflect on your feelings for them.

Practice being nurturing with those around you rather than letting others take care of your needs all the time.

14
TWO PEAS IN A POD: TWINS

In form and feature, face and limb,
I grew so like my brother,
That folks got taking me for him
And each for one another.
It puzzled all our kith and kin,
It reached a fearful pitch;
For one of us was born a twin
And not a soul knew which.

...I put this question, fruitlessly,
To every one I knew,
"What would you do, if you were me,
To prove that you were you?

Our close resemblance turned the tide
Of my domestic life,
For somehow, my intended bride
Became my brother's wife.
In fact, year after year the same
Absurd mistakes went on,
And when I died — the neighbors came
And buried brother John.

Henry Sambroke Leigh, "The Twins"

Twins are an object of fascination and wonder for most people — even their parents. Unless separated at birth, their entire childhood, as well as prenatal, experience is affected by being a twin. Identical twins share common genes and therefore have constitutional similarities, but much of their development depends on how their parents have thought about and dealt with having twins.

a. PHYSIOLOGY OF TWINSHIP

No one decides to have twins; having twins happens involuntarily, although some women know they are "at risk" because of taking fertility drugs (which increase the chances of multiple births) or because of a history of twins in their family. Twins occur about once in every 90 births for whites and once in every 70 births for blacks. The myth of twin births skipping a generation has fooled many a woman who had twins just as her mother did.

Ultrasound scanning is revealing new information about twins, including the fact that many single children start out as twins but one is lost in the early stages of pregnancy — unbeknownst to the mother. Early scans of pregnant women have shown two fetuses, one of which then disappears in later scans. Early bleeding in pregnancy, with no other ill effects, can be an indication of the loss of a twin fetus. The evidence is that twice as many twins are conceived as are born.

Whether twins are fraternal or identical has an immense impact on the way they develop as human beings. Fraternal twins are the result of the woman releasing two eggs in one month, which are each fertilized by a different sperm. The eggs implant themselves in the wall of the uterus close or far apart. If far apart, they each have completely separate outer sacs and placentas. If they are very close together, their outer sacs and placentas may fuse, but the fetuses are still completely different genetically. Like any other two siblings, they can closely resemble each other or look nothing alike. They can be two boys, two girls, or a boy and a girl. Fraternal twins never look exactly the same, and boy-girl twins are never identical twins.

Identical twins are the result of one egg being fertilized by one sperm and then dividing so that both fetuses have exactly the same genes. How close they are in the womb depends on the stage at which the egg divides. If the egg divides very early, each fetus will have its own outer sac and placenta; if the egg divides late, they will share the same amniotic sac.

About one third of all twins are identical. Half are girl pairs and half boy pairs. They are physically identical in every way, from the same blood to the same skin, although some markings may be mirror-image — that is, a mole on the left side of one twin's face may be in the same place but on the right side of the other twin's.

The possibility of having twins increases with each birth. Twins are more likely to occur as a woman ages, with the mid-thirties the peak time. A woman of 40 is more likely to have twins than a woman of 20, so twins are usually the youngests in their family. Most couples seem to stop having children after they have had twins, or they wait at least four or five years before having another child.

b. REACTION OF PARENTS

Husbands and wives have mixed feelings when they learn they will have twins. Some are overjoyed; some are just overwhelmed. Some think they are getting "two for the price of one" and enjoy the extra attention and acclaim they receive. Some are horrified and feel unable to cope. The earlier in the pregnancy the couple find out, the better their adjustment. Before ultrasound scanning was commonly used, the advent of twins was often a surprise late in the pregnancy or even at the birth, which was a shock, to say the least. So for many twins, just the fact of unexpectedly being one too many creates a different atmosphere in the home than they would have had as singles.

For other twins, the added anxiety of their parents starts before birth when the mother may worry, legitimately, that one will die in the womb or that she will not be able to carry them long enough for both to be healthy and whole. And indeed, most twins are born earlier and with a lower birth weight than singles and have to spend time in an incubator or a neonatal unit rather than being with the mother and going home in a few days.

Parents are not usually as closely tied to their twins as they are to their other children. The lack of close contact after birth can affect the early bonding process and add to the sense of distance between parents and twins.

Newborn twins often look stranger than single babies — extremely skinny and wrinkled and pushed out of shape. Because they came on the scene earlier, premature babies are, naturally, less socially responsive to the parents and take longer to react in satisfying ways with a smile or recognition of mother's face. As a result, the relationship with adults may be tenuous from the beginning.

It is also more difficult for anybody to develop two intense love relationships simultaneously, so it may take longer for parents to feel as loving toward their twins as toward their other children. In the case of identical twins, the problem is compounded by the difficulty in telling them apart. Parents may not know who it is they're loving at the moment.

Twins often benefit from the more active involvement of father in their care. The sheer magnitude of the job of taking care of twins means that most fathers *have* to help with feeding, diapering, and washing to a greater extent than they do with single babies.

The idea of being a twin has a tremendous appeal for people who wish for a soul mate to know and love and support them in exactly the way they want to be known, loved, and supported. If these people become the parents of twins, they see their fantasy being fulfilled in their children. These are the parents most likely to play up the twin phenomenon by dressing the children alike and treating them as though they are exactly the same person.

Bess, who was the fifth of six children, had a sister who was just eleven months younger. They were so close in age to each other and there was such a large age gap between them and the fourth child that they became a natural sub-group. Early in their life, the whole family began to refer to them together as "the babies" and "the twins," and they began to lose their separate identities. They both had blond curly hair and hazel eyes and often dressed in identical clothes. As children and as adolescents they enjoyed their special relationship, the attention they got for being so alike and so cute, and the mutual support they gave each other.

But in her late twenties, Bess began to have problems with this twin-like identity. Her family, friends, employer, co-workers, and, to some extent, her husband did not take her as seriously as she wished they would. She began to be uncomfortable with her way of getting things by being "cute" and helpless. The family still referred to Bess and her sister as "the twins." She didn't like their assumption that whatever her sister said was true of her also.

She had tried, in a number of ways, to tell people "I'm not a twin and I'm not a baby," but this only seemed to intensify both her relationship problems (she was perceived as having a childish tantrum) and her feelings of unhappiness. In therapy she learned to stop trying to change others and to start thinking about how she wanted to change her behavior with them. This required that she let go of some of her manipulative tricks (which got her the help she desired but reinforced her image as one of the twin babies).

She also needed to be more open and direct in expressing her own opinions and more adult in paying attention to family members and their needs rather than trying to get all the attention for herself and her problems. As she worked on this, much to her satisfaction, she began to get feedback from family members who said in admiration that "Bess is really growing up" and "has a mind of her own."

It just so happened that the year after she stopped therapy, Bess gave birth to identical twins. She was adamant that she and her husband would not treat them as "the twins." She intended to dress and groom each child differently and appreciate whatever differences began to emerge between them.

c. THE TWINS' BIRTH ORDER CHARACTERISTICS

If there are no other children in the family, twins will act like two siblings of whatever sex they are, without the age conflict. They will both have some of the characteristics of the youngest and oldest of their sex. In families where the parents emphasize that one was born before the other (even if just by a few minutes, but particularly if there are several hours between the births), the older one may take the role of the oldest and treat the hours-younger twin like a younger sibling. Or they may take on oldest-youngest roles according to size if they are fraternal twins and one has a larger build than the other.

When there are other children in the family, the twins will both have most of the characteristics of the birth position they share. For example, if the twin boys are the youngest in a family of girls, they will each be a lot like a single youngest brother of sisters in addition to their unique characteristics as twins.

Since twins are usually the last children in their family, they share the exceedingly special position of being the babies and also being "unusual." They may be doubly fussed over and spoiled as a result, especially by people outside the family. Parents of twins are kept so busy with the physical tasks of caring for two babies that they are unable to pay as much attention to each twin as they did to their older children. Older children can be more accepting of twins for this reason and also because they get some notoriety for having twins in their family. However, a single older sibling who has not had to compete for attention previously and feels outnumbered by the two newcomers may give up trying to get attention and fade into the background — or may try to get attention in anti-social ways, becoming the "delinquent," thus distorting the usual birth order characteristics for all positions in that family.

When twins are followed by a single baby several years later, that younger sibling is often very much enjoyed by the mother who finds the single so easy to care for in comparison to the twins. She may luxuriate in this child and pay even less attention to the twins. However, the twins may be so wrapped up in their own little world by that time that they won't notice.

See the other chapters on each birth order for a description of the position each twin has in the family relative to other siblings.

d. PERSONALITY DEVELOPMENT

Preschooler twins spend almost 24 hours a day together, much more time than they spend with even their mother, so their greatest influence is on each other. Since they are at every stage of life equally knowledgeable and, therefore, unlikely to push or pull each other along in development, they tend to be slower in developing and later in achievement.

Twins also usually have less parental pressure to achieve than other children. Parents just don't have as much time to worry over every little thing and measure progress in the same way. The parents aren't readily able to track each individual's behavior so they tend to be inconsistent in disciplining twins and in praising them to reinforce skill development. Twins are ignored or told "no" by their parents more often than other birth orders, and they also more easily ignore commands from their parents since, unless they are addressed individually, they can each pretend the message is meant for the other twin.

Studies have shown that parents talk less to their twins and, because of all the distractions, respond less to the twins' talk. Because they imitate each other's speech more than adult speech, twins are usually slower to talk intelligibly. The stories of private languages developed by twins, however, are exaggerated. They usually use only a few words that others can't understand, although mother usually does. Most twins do not intend to be secretive, they just have less need to say words correctly since they understand each other. They may also use more shortcuts in talking by leaving out articles and verbs. They catch up with other children in their speaking abilities as soon as they go to school and have to make themselves understood to others.

However, throughout their school days, twins continue to score the lowest of all birth positions in intelligence tests and often don't try very hard to excel or develop any area of expertise. Just being "a twin act" makes them special enough, particularly if the parents have emphasized the twinship. Very few famous people are identical twins.

Twins are also less willing than others to pay attention to and learn from elders, whether siblings, parents, or teachers. They are too much their own little team. In fact, other siblings or classmates may have little to do with them. Twins rely on each other for so much that they may not make the effort to get along with others. They deeply believe in "united we stand, divided we fall."

They are particularly adept at using their double power over their mother. They can often wear her down simply by being able to outnumber her. Two beings claiming their rights can be more persuasive than one when they declare, "We don't want to take a nap."

Girl twins, both identical and fraternal, are usually more outgoing than boy twins. They are also less competitive with each other than boy twins and seem to get more enjoyment out of being a twin, perhaps because people admire them more in their fancy dresses and so forth. Of all family members, girl twins develop the closest and longest-lasting relationships with each other. Abigail Van Buren (Dear Abby) and identical twin Ann Landers spent every day together until their double wedding. After a period of estrangement, they now fax each other several times every day if they are not visiting and talking through the night, sharing the same bed.

e. THE CLOSENESS OF TWINS

All twins are unusually close to each other, and if they are identical, they often act as one person. As young children, they may not know who is who and think they are each other at times. Even adult identical twins living apart can have the experience of seeing themselves unexpectedly in a mirror and thinking their twin has come into the room.

Twins are thrown together from prenatal times on and are left to their own devices more than other children. Busy parents are usually happy for the respite they get when they can put the two babies together to entertain each other. Twins can be even more isolated than only children since their parents feel less need to involve them with children outside the family. If the twins are always together when they are with other children, they may not know whose friends are whose or may suspect that other children are friendly with them just for the novelty value.

Thus, they have seldom experienced the world without their twin and may feel their twin is the only really trustworthy person around. They become mutually dependent on always having the other around to see them through life's ups and downs. Their experience is completely unlike any other sibling type. Whereas most siblings are eager to put distance between them when young, twins (especially identical twins) are threatened by too much distance from their twin. They depend on each other being there to help make sense of the world.

> The narcissistic advantages of being a twin are a major factor that is intuitively appreciated by non-twins who typically envy twins their constant companionship, which they imagine to be totally without ambivalence. Such narcissism constitutes a powerful force working against achieving separateness. For us, the narcissistic gain of being twins was reinforced early in childhood, as well as by family, and, later on, by the extraordinary power we felt in our ability to deceive others.
>
> Twin George L. Engel,
> quoted in *The Sibling Bond*

It is often difficult for twins to marry. The intimacy of marriage is a pale imitation of the intimacy of twinship and rarely satisfies a twin's need for emotional closeness. Even male/female twins have trouble separating, though they are at least used to a close peer of the opposite sex so will find in marriage a familiar arrangement. But opposite-sex twins often experience jealousy when a twin starts dating or marries.

Identical twins have the most difficulty separating. They, even more than other twins, want to and often do marry twins. Sometimes, they may share one lover or friend without conflict because they think of themselves as one person. The movie *Dead Ringers* was an example of this tendency carried to monstrous extremes — male twin gynecologists tricked patients and lovers by trading places with each other in a sadistic way.

The extreme need for closeness is a threat to many marriages that involve a twin. Rachel, 26, complained in her first counseling session that her husband did not understand her, did not support her emotionally, did not talk to her enough, and was just too distant. For the past five years, she had been having fairly strong anxiety attacks, which were beginning to inhibit her ability to work, and she wanted to see if there was a connection.

The therapist found out that Rachel was an identical twin and had never been separated from her twin sister for any length of time until the end of university, when they were 21. Rachel thought of her sister Rochelle as being a more capable and competent person than she was and had always depended on Rochelle to take care of her; they spent hours together talking over experiences and problems. Rachel had married within six months of graduating from university. Her anxiety attacks could be traced back to the time of separation from her sister, and it began to be clear to her that she was expecting her husband to provide the kind of closeness and companionship she had been used to with her sister — something that was impossible to replicate.

Her husband Hendrick, it turned out, was an only child. Twins and only children, of all the sibling positions, have the least in common in terms of their experience of life and family. They represent the opposite extremes of togetherness and separateness. However, Rachel had been attracted to Hendrick's independence and self-assurance, and he was attracted to Rachel's warmth and openness and ability to relate. However, since he lacked these qualities himself, he was not able to reciprocate with the kind of closeness she wanted. He could see that it might be a good idea — he just did not have the internal emotional resources and the life experience to do it. And Rachel's years of twin togetherness made it too difficult for her to learn to accept Hendrick's emotional distance and more private style.

They finally decided to divorce. Because they made this decision while they were in therapy and had discovered and understood the factors that contributed to their difficulties, they were able to separate in a caring way. They have remained friends even though both have remarried.

f.   SPECIAL CHALLENGES FOR TWINS

As *Dead Ringers* also showed, twins are not necessarily alike emotionally. In their efforts to be valued as individuals as they grow up, some twins may work very hard at being different from each other. One twin study found that identical twins reared apart were more alike than the ones brought up together.

Twins raised together may take on different roles and be encouraged in that by others to such an extent that if one twin does well in something the other twin gives up any attempt even to be competent or functional in that area. For example, one twin may be labelled by parents as the social one and the other twin will withdraw completely into being the quiet one so that they remain two halves of a whole. They may, by their own volition, take on complementary characteristics so that one is smart and the other dumb or one serious and one playful and then switch roles once or several times during their growing-up years.

Because twins are, unfortunately, often expected to share everything from a crib to a bicycle, fairness is a big issue for many adult twins. They are overly sensitive to any slight or the appearance of being given less time, less attention, less money than someone else. Possessions and ownership become overly important to them. As youngsters they do not share willingly, and because they know each other's tactics so well they find more creative ways to avoid sharing and are more troublesome about it than other siblings who have to share. Because twins are so close and so dependent on each other, they may feel especially guilty about not wanting to share. This guilt can add to their hostility when they are asked to share all the time. They love their twin — but they hate that grabby twin too. The added implication of self-love and self-hate complicates these emotions.

He is my most beloved friend and my bitterest rival, my confidant and my betrayer, my sustainer and my dependent, and scariest of all, my equal.

Gregg Levoy, writing about his twin in
Psychology Today, June, 1989

Twins who are treated as individuals rather than as "twins" from birth onward are more likely to be well-rounded as adults and function well on their own in the world. Even the names of twins can affect this ability to think of themselves as individuals. Twins whose names are too much alike (Jim and Tim, Jean and Joan) or have the same origin (Hope and Charity) are more easily confused by others as youngsters and more likely to think of themselves as half of a whole.

Twins who have had the luxury of always having separate rooms and being dressed and treated differently have fewer of the twin traits and more of the traits of their position in the family relative to other children. If a twin has developed a closer relationship with another sibling, that twin will be more influenced by his or her birth order in relation to that sibling. When twin Jennie was two years old, she was "adopted" by her six-year-old sister and thus developed more of the characteristics of a youngest sister of sisters than did her fraternal twin Martha.

Older sisters in a family seem to be more accepting of younger twins than older brothers are. A single older sibling may feel ganged up on by the "terrible twosome" and need special protection for his or her threatened possessions and position in the family. In some cases, parents send their twins to a different school from the older sibling's to allow the older child some exclusive territory not subject to invasion from below.

Regardless of how well they have done at being individuals, the loss of the twin is the greatest loss in the world for a twin, worse than the loss of parent, spouse, or child. It is as though they have lost part of themselves. Some react neurotically to the death of their twin by refusing to acknowledge the fact that they ever were a twin.

The death of a twin at birth can also affect the surviving twin. The parents who were expecting twins may feel as though they have only half a child and much of their psychic energy may go into grieving for the lost twin rather than bonding with the living twin. They may also feel at some level that celebrating the birth of one twin is being disloyal to the dead twin, so they withdraw to some extent. This may be even truer for parents who were unhappy or ambivalent about the prospect of twins and are then racked by guilt when one dies.

Some parents react to the infant death of a twin by being overprotective of the survivor or treating the survivor as a twin even though the child has no awareness or experience of being a twin.

g. TO THE PARENTS OF TWINS

While being a twin can be a unique and wonderful thing during childhood, it is not always good preparation for the next 65 years of adult life.

Try to think of your twins as two individuals who just happen to be the same age and may look the same. Remember that what is cute at 6 months may not be cute at 16 or 60 years. In addition to dressing them differently, think of them and address them by their individual names rather than as "the twins."

In your effort to treat them equally, don't always treat them the same. If one toddler wants a $2 coloring book and the other wants a $20 truck, don't insist that the expenditure be equal. They don't know about monetary values. Just let them choose according to their different interests, and support these as they begin to emerge.

Respond to each child's needs individually. If one needs more cuddling, don't impose it on the other, who may need more roughhouse playing. When they are older, try to arrange to take them out separately and have them play with other children separately — as much as the mindboggling logistics permit. Your own health and happiness is the most important aspect of their upbringing, so that has to come first. Be sure to ask for help from others when you need it, and spend time alone as a couple, doing the things you enjoy together.

Try to encourage others — teachers and relatives — to recognize each twin as an individual. For instance, ask people to send separate birthday cards to each one, not one card to "the twins." When taking them into new situations — a school, a swimming class — take them separately, just as you would your children of different ages, to introduce them first as individuals, before they become known as twins.

15
EXCEPTIONS AND VARIATIONS: FACTORS THAT ALTER THE USUAL TRAITS OF BIRTH ORDER AND SEX

My mother loved children — she would have given anything if I had been one.

Groucho Marx

Sometimes factors or events in a family severely disrupt the usual developmental patterns of the children. In those cases, the children are less likely to have the personality traits commonly exhibited by others of their birth order and sex.

These out-of-the-ordinary factors usually involve some difficulty in the family, such as the early death of a parent or of a sibling, or great emotional intensity in the family. Both of these situations would alter the personality patterns of one or more of the children in the family.

The variations can also be caused by more positive departures from the average family functioning. For instance, parents who have overcome their own sex-role stereotyping enough may influence that aspect of their children's development. Their daughters, for example, will be more ambitious or more career-oriented than most women of their birth order position.

An extremely well functioning family may produce children who do not share some of the negative characteristics of others in their birth order and gender position. In addition, an adult who has experienced quite a bit of personal growth may have gone beyond the childhood limitations of his or her birth order and gender.

A strong identification with the same-sex parent also influences the development of the usual characteristics. For example, a younger brother of sisters who tries hard to emulate his father who is an older brother of brothers may have more characteristics associated with older brothers of brothers than with his own birth order position.

However, deviations from the standard descriptions of birth order position are more often caused by disturbances in the family. It is important to be aware of this when looking at ways you might want to change your current functioning. Since birth order characteristics are basically set by age five, the younger the children when the disturbance occurs, the more likely it is to have an effect. Later changes in the family's life will modify the characteristics but not alter them significantly.

a. LOSS OF PARENTS IN CHILDHOOD

The loss of a parent in early childhood (up to about six years old) has such a severe impact on children that it can drastically alter the development of the typical characteristics for their birth order and gender. Oldest children in that age range are usually affected most by loss of a parent. They are more aware of what is happening and they have also had a longer experience of living in an intact family so are likely to miss it more.

They may, for example, regress in their behavior as a way to get back to the early, good times.

The very young child (under six months) does not experience the loss directly, but feels over the years the effects of how others in the family experienced the loss. This loss becomes significant if there is no one else to provide the nurturing and play the protective-parent role.

The loss might be because of death, divorce, war, extended work demands away from home, or hospitalization. The functional incapacity of a parent who is still physically present but no longer able to act as a parent due to physical or emotional disabilities is felt as a loss. An addictive or abusive parent unable to provide a sense of safety or nurture is also experienced as a loss.

In the case of a death, and sometimes in a divorce, the remaining parent may be so grief-stricken that he or she is unable to offer the solace and reassurance the grieving child needs, so the child keeps these feelings bottled up, sometimes for decades. The effect of the loss, even when unrecognized or unacknowledged, can have a far-reaching impact on every aspect of the person's later life.

This early loss can create an insecurity and fear of the future that is disproportionate to the actual events of the rest of the child's life. This fear alters the usual birth order characteristics and thus the way this person relates to others. For example, youngest sisters of brothers usually relate well to men and choose men who are likely to be good mates for them, but if they have lost a parent early in life they are more likely to choose later partners unwisely. There is a hidden compulsion to repeat the loss, which may have been perceived as punishment, because that is what they have experienced with loved ones. They tend to choose people who are likely to leave them or cause them pain in some way. This may have been the case with Lady Bird Johnson, who put up with quite a bit from Lyndon Johnson. A youngest child with two much older brothers, her mother died when she was five and she went to live alone with an unmarried aunt.

Often, people who have had an early loss will end up with a spouse who has also had an early loss, and both of them will have the expectation that "loved ones end up hurting you" (i.e., leaving you). They will then expect and even provoke that behavior from each other. This is not done deliberately out of a masochistic need for pain, but because it is the familiar feeling and they know how to play that particular role of being "the abandoned one."

Maintaining an ongoing, lasting, emotionally stable relationship is not something they know how to do from early experience. In spite of wishing it were otherwise, these people are often more comfortable with the actual loss than with the uncertainty of not knowing when a loss might occur again and their uneasiness in staying in an ongoing relationship.

1. Death of a parent

A universal characteristic of young children is their belief that the world began when they were born and that the world revolves around them. This not only gives them a sense of power — however unrealistic — but also leads them to think that whatever happens is their responsibility. They are unable to conceive of their parents and others as having separate existences influenced by things beyond the child's awareness.

Given their egocentric view of the world, young children often assume that the death of a parent is a punishment, no matter how undeserved it may be. This feeling can help establish a pattern of underlying depression that will overshadow the usual birth order traits.

Children can also feel guilty about "causing" the death of a parent. Since young children often think they are omnipotent, they may fear that their occasional normal angry wish that the parent was gone (which is what death means to them) caused the parent to die or leave. Among other things, this guilt contributes to a feeling of worthlessness and perhaps bitterness in these children, which may not usually be present in children of their birth order.

Children may also, in their magical way of thinking, believe that the parent left them (died) because of their bad behavior. This could cause a normally rambunctious, or "bad," younger child to become subdued and passive. Or a normally well-behaved older child could just give up trying to be good since "it didn't help," and start misbehaving.

Sometimes, the death of a parent causes siblings to become closer. The children may turn to each other, particularly if the remaining parent is unavailable emotionally. They may feel more dependent on each other and lose some of their competitive feelings, or at least bury them for the sake of present comfort. Those who are near the same age may wordlessly comfort each other. Those who have a much older sibling may turn to that sibling for help, which often works well for both if the parents had modelled loving behavior that the older sibling can imitate.

Richard Burton was two years old when his mother died in childbirth (with her thirteenth child). He was sent to live with his married oldest sister who became his mother in every way. As it happened, her husband's sister and son lived in the same house. The son was the same age as Richard, and they grew up as close "brothers."

Just as often, however, the death of a parent can create greater dissension among the siblings, causing an even greater deviation in their birth order traits. The oldest sibling may become more than usually hostile toward the younger siblings, acting out of his or her own anger at death and fear of being abandoned.

When people experience an important loss, it is normal for them to develop some kind of pattern of compensation. These patterns can be in negative or positive directions. Psychologist Walter Toman found that people in jail and people who were psychologically disturbed had lost their mothers when very young significantly more often than people in the general population. At the other extreme, anecdotal evidence suggests that many famous "successful" people, from business magnates to philosophers to actors, suffered a severe early loss of some kind.

2.   Divorce

Divorce is always experienced as a loss by children, even if it is the best solution for the parents. If the non-custodial parent stays in close touch and the couple can work well together as parents, the effects on the child's development are less severe. If the divorced parent loses contact with the child or the parents continue fighting with each other, the child is more likely to suffer a long-lasting impact, as in a death.

In all cases, divorce is a crisis in the family. The "voluntary" leaving of one parent can seem extremely threatening to young children who think that they are the cause of everything that happens. As in a death, they can feel guilt for wishing it at some level. When a son secretly feels he'd be happier if he didn't have to share mother with his father and father then leaves, that young boy may feel responsible and act up out of guilt. He may also feel disillusioned and angry when his fantasy of how good it would be not to share mother is crushed by the reality of mother being distracted and upset by the divorce and having even less time available to spend with him alone.

The insecurity caused by the divorce — especially if it has been preceded by years of angry wrangling and followed by years of bitterness — can exacerbate the normal sibling rivalry. The children may react with increased jealousy between them as they juggle more ferociously for position with the remaining parent or with the more rarely seen absent parent. It becomes even more important to them to get their fair share of the reduced parental attention that is available. The patterns of birth order may then become more entrenched and exaggerated, with the oldest becoming more obsessive and more domineering and the youngest more rebellious and more irresponsible.

Siblings can also blame each other for the departure of the parent and become more than ordinarily hostile toward each other. And if their parents continue fighting after the divorce and use the children as weapons, the children may be forced into taking sides and end up fighting their parents' battles with each other.

In some cases, a divorce splits up the siblings when some go to live with their father and others stay with mother. More often an older boy will go with father while the younger siblings stay with mother. This changes their sibling position in the family, which has a greater effect the earlier it occurs. For example, if a 10-year-old middle boy suddenly becomes the oldest because his 13-year-old brother goes to live with the father, his characteristics are well enough set that he is less likely to take on the traits of an oldest at that point. But if the move occurs when he is four years old, there is a much better chance that he will develop more oldest son characteristics.

b. REMARRIAGE

When adults who have children from previous marriages remarry, they create a whole new family constellation by "blending" together their separate families. As more and more North Americans divorce, the number of remarriages is increasing.

The possible variations in the makeup of the new family are numerous. In decreasing order of the impact they have on the children's birth order characteristics, they are:

(a) Both spouses have children and all the children live with them

(b) Both spouses have children, but only one set lives with them; the other set visits on weekends or other specific times

(c) Only one spouse has children and the children live with them

(d) Only one spouse has children and they only visit

Within those categories, the children may all be young, all old, both young and old, all of one sex or mixed sexes, and so on.

In general, these "blended families" do not usually blend very well. It is common for a step-parent or a step-sibling to become the target of one child's anger about the divorce or death of a parent. A step-parent or a step-sibling may also be seen as further competition for the remaining parent's love and reacted against strongly. Just the fact of the divorce and remarriage is disruption enough for children, but if they also have to adjust to additional children in the family, they are likely to have a struggle.

Parents tend to see remarriage as a gain for their children, especially if the children have lost touch with the non-custodial parent. But the majority of children experience a parent's remarriage as a further loss. They not only have to share their family life with others (seen as intruders) but the parent is now devoting a lot of time and attention to the new spouse. The remarriage also ends the normal hope that most children of divorce have that their parents will get back together. The new marriage is blamed for making this impossible.

The younger the children are when they become part of the new family, the greater the effect will be on the normal development of their birth order characteristics. Children older than two usually keep their original birth order characteristics but may add new ones as a result of their change in status. Younger children are more likely to acquire all new characteristics if their place in the family changes. A one-year-old girl who acquires an older step-sister will be more likely to develop the characteristics of a youngest sister of sisters than a six-year-old girl will.

Most divorces occur when the youngest child is a teenager, so when a remarriage occurs for those families, it has less impact on the birth order characteristics.

When step-siblings live together in the same house, their birth order position becomes more confused than if one set just visits on weekends. The adjustment to the new family arrangement is easier and the effect on birth order traits less noticeable when the step-siblings are separated by a number of years. If one set is much older than the other set, there is likely to be less interaction. Each set usually sticks together and maintains their own order of birth within their group. When Derek, 15, and Alan, 13, moved in with their step-siblings, Jon, 4, and Joy, 3, they had very little to do with the younger children and were set enough in their own personalities that they maintained their oldest brother and youngest brother of brothers characteristics intact.

However, when the ages are closer together and the children are younger, more changes in the usual birth order traits are likely. When Ann-Lou, 6, and Lilly, 8, went to live with Shona, 4, and Billy-Joe, 2, it did affect their birth order traits. Ann-Lou was no longer the youngest, but an older middle. With two less capable children around, she felt more grown-up and began to be bossier. Both older girls felt motherly toward young Billy-Joe and competed over taking care of him, and as a result developed some characteristics of an oldest sister of a brother.

Oldest children often have more difficulty if a step-sibling who is also the oldest is near the same age. Neither wants to give up being the leader of the children and having the most privileges. The conflict between them can aggravate their negative characteristics or cause one of them to regress.

The two youngests from each set may also have conflicts if they are close in age. Neither wants to give up the special position of the baby, and neither is able to lord it over anyone else as might have been possible if a much younger sibling had been added to the family.

Sometimes, when all goes well, the step-siblings become friends and can learn from each other. Single-sex siblings who have opposite-sex step-siblings can learn about living with opposite-sex peers. Opposite-sex step-siblings usually get along better than same-sex step-siblings, sometimes so well that it causes concern for the parents who want to extend the incest taboo to step-siblings.

If an only child joins a family with several children, the only may be overwhelmed by the step-siblings to such an extent that the only child characteristics are greatly altered. The only who becomes the oldest of the siblings may become very much like an oldest, growing either bossy and domineering or more nurturing. An only who becomes the youngest or middle child is more likely to maintain the only-child characteristics and think of the step-siblings as additional parents.

If the remarried parents also have children together, it creates another level of relatedness in the family and adds increased possibilities for jealousy and resentment. All of the step-siblings will be half-siblings to the new child. They may feel threatened by the new baby unless they are much older or very young themselves. The youngest in the existing family is likely to feel the effects of the half-sibling the most and may react negatively.

If the new baby is the first biological child for the mother, she may treat the baby like a firstborn, so this child will grow up with oldest child characteristics even though he or she is the youngest child of the remarried couple.

Sigmund Freud was his father's fifth child, but the first of six children of his mother who was his father's second wife. Sigmund's mother was convinced "from the moment of his birth" that he had been "born to fulfill a high destiny." Despite the four older half-siblings, he was much more like an oldest than a middle child.

Frank Lloyd Wright also was the fourth child of his widowed father, but the first biological child of his mother's. While she was pregnant, she read books about cathedrals and hoped for a boy who would become a famous architect. In typical first-born style, he did.

If the new baby is the first boy in the family, he may be treated more like an oldest by both parents since he is the oldest boy as well as their oldest joint child.

Occasionally, the birth of a new baby has a solidifying effect on the family. The baby is seen by the other children as a sign that the family arrangement is going to be permanent, which may have a calming effect on them. In this case, they are likely to welcome the half-sibling as a full sibling, and develop their birth order characteristics accordingly.

c. DEATH OF A SIBLING

The early loss of an older sibling may feel similar to the loss of a parent for a young child and have similar repercussions.

The death of an older sibling usually has a more profound effect than the death of a younger sibling. The older sibling, like a parent, has always been there, while a younger sibling was not always part of the family and in the fewer years he or she was alive probably had less influence on the older siblings.

People who have lost a sibling in childhood are less likely to marry and less likely to have children of their own, recent studies have shown. As with the loss of a parent, they don't want to take the risk of getting close to someone who will then "abandon" them.

Also, as in the death of a parent, children often feel at fault if a sibling dies. They are even more likely to have wished in angry moments for a sibling's death or disappearance and to have mixed feelings about the loss. Their guilt can cause them to react in ways that change their usual birth order characteristics. They may try to take the place of the sibling to make it up to the parents or go the opposite way and be as different and as difficult as possible.

Sometimes the guilt they feel is survivor's guilt. They wonder why the sibling had to die and why they were "allowed" to live, undeserving as they are. That guilt and a buried fear that maybe they too will die can disturb the normal development of birth order characteristics.

If the oldest sibling dies, the next oldest child often tries to fill the role of the oldest and will take on those characteristics to some extent. This is especially likely if they are close in age and the death happens when they are young, but it can happen even later in life.

The Kennedy family clearly illustrates this. John F. Kennedy, as the second oldest boy in the family, was not on the same pedestal as his older brother. The biography *The Fitzgeralds and the Kennedys: An American Saga* describes how Joe Junior "was accorded an initial position of primacy which he then built upon as a consequence of his temperament... he emanated power, passion and promise... a conquering poise that made him seem older." But Joe died when John was 27, and John quickly took on the mantle of oldest, highest-achieving male in the family. The rest of the family looked to him to fill that role. When John Kennedy died, Robert Kennedy stepped in. When Robert died, Teddy Kennedy tried to step in, but his youngest son characteristics have made it difficult for him to assume the role of oldest and to project the kind of responsible style expected of presidents.

The way the parents handle the death of their child makes a big difference in what happens to the remaining children. If the parents make a saint of the dead child, the ones left may feel that they can never live up to that ideal or compete successfully. They may give up completely and become underachievers or depressed, when their usual birth order traits would make them high achievers or happy children.

The parents may be so pre-occupied with their own grief that they lose interest in the remaining children, who then have the doubly painful experience of losing a sibling and the attention of their parents at the same time. They may, in fact, actually lose a parent too, as the incidence of divorce following a child's death is higher than average.

The parents may react to the death in another, equally disturbing way. They may become overly protective and restrictive with the surviving children or cling to them for emotional support, all of which will interfere with the usual patterns of development for the children.

John Paul Getty's older sister died at age 10 before he was born. At his birth, his mother became "determined that this child would not be allowed to die. He would be guarded from the possibility of infection by a possessive overprotective mother, yet John Paul was never given any physical affection," says biographer Robert Lenzner. Relatives theorized that the death of his sister made his mother afraid to love and cuddle him too much.

A child born after the death of another child or after a miscarriage or stillbirth often takes on a special significance in the family. The parents may, for example, take extra precautions with the next child born alive and focus more attention and care on that child than would be expected. As a result, a youngest child may end up having a childhood that is as closely monitored as the first child's, thus changing the usual outcome for a youngest's personality.

If the first child dies before others are born but still has a strong ghostlike presence in the family, the next child — the first living child — may act like a younger child rather than an oldest without anyone knowing why.

On March 30, 1852, a first child was born to the Van Goghs in Holland. He was named Vincent, and he died after a few weeks. On March 30, 1853, another baby boy was born to the same mother. He also was named Vincent. He was brought up knowing "that in the eyes of his mother he was but a shadowy substitute for that other Vincent who had died. He felt unwanted." Vincent had little connection with his three younger sisters, but as an adult became dependent on his younger brother Theo, who often supported him financially as well as emotionally.

A child born after the death of any of the children may have transferred to it some of the role of the dead child. Characteristics associated with the deceased child may be projected onto the baby who is seen as taking the place of the dead child. In this way a youngest child might become more like the oldest child who died, while the second oldest maintains the middle position.

Golda Meir was the eighth child in her family, but six of her older siblings died in childhood, so she was highly prized after so many deaths. With more than nine years between her and the oldest daughter, she became more like an oldest herself with the birth of her younger sister.

The death of a middle child can create a large enough age gap between the remaining siblings that they form sub-groups and so develop birth order traits that reflect their position in the sub-group. When seven-year-old Shelley died, she left an age gap between the four remaining children. Twelve-year-old Sean and ten-year-old Iris formed one group and, with a greater impact on them because they were younger, four-year-old Sandie and two-year-old Stevie formed another group. Sandie was now the oldest in her sub-group and developed more oldest child characteristics than would have been expected.

The gap between sub-groups can also create a youngest child who functions as an only child. This occurs frequently when a child's conception is considered a mistake by parents who had their "last" child a number of years before and thought they were beyond all that.

The sudden death of a sibling — or a suicidal or violent death — further complicates the situation and makes it even more unlikely that the remaining children will have the usual characteristics of their birth order. The increase in teen suicides and drug deaths in recent years makes this an increasingly widespread issue for the next generation of adults.

When middle child Katharine Hepburn was 10 years old, she found her older brother hanged to death; she changed from a "carefree tomboy to a moody, nervous, distrustful child," says biographer Charles Higham.

d. DEATH OF OTHER FAMILY MEMBERS

Even the death of non-nuclear family members can have an impact on the children of the family, particularly when it is a relative one of the parents was closely tied to emotionally.

One of the children is often "designated" as the replacement for the deceased. This often becomes the function of a child born shortly after a significant death in the family.

If the parent was dependent emotionally on the deceased, the child could become a "parental child" and feel responsible for taking care of the parent. If the parent's feelings toward the deceased were hostile, the same battles might be repeated with the child. One piece of research showed that children who were eventually diagnosed as "schizophrenic" when they were young adults had a grandparent who died within one year, on either side, of their birth.

e. ADOPTION

Birth order characteristics are only relevant in the context of the family you are raised in. A child may be the youngest child of the biological mother, but if adopted at birth and raised as the oldest child in the adoptive family, the child will have the characteristics of an oldest, not a youngest, child.

One effect adoption sometimes has is to increase the level of anxiety in the parents and intensify their efforts to do "a good job." Thus, an adopted child who is the youngest child in the family may receive the same kind of parenting that the oldest child did and develop many oldest child characteristics.

Adoptive parents are generally from a higher class and income level than average, which adds to the pressure on the child to turn out well and succeed. Sometimes, adoptive parents also have a need to prove to the world that their adopted children are "as good as" the biological children of their friends. In this case, they tend to push the child harder than would be expected. The birth order traits of adopted children in the middle and youngest positions in particular can be affected by this.

If the parents adopt a baby as their first child after several years of trying to have their own baby, they are even more likely to be nervous about parenting. They may not have had much notice before the baby became available and may be less prepared emotionally and physically to deal with a baby than a couple who has had nine months and a lot of hormones to get them ready. These parents may be exceptionally protective and careful with this baby, and if they subsequently have one of their own, which seems to happen frequently, they may greet that one with much relief and be even more relaxed than parents usually are with their second. The oldest and youngest child characteristics of these two children may be accentuated to a point of distortion.

Parents who have an adopted first child and a biological second child sometimes get alarmed that their biological child seems to be slower in developing. They do not realize that this is a natural result of birth order. They may end up unconsciously trying harder with the second child and this can make the second child, whether a middle or youngest, seem more like an oldest child. This can also happen if the parents consider their biological child to be their "real" child and invest more of themselves in pushing this child.

If the adoption takes place later in childhood, the child's original birth order characteristics will be modified somewhat by whatever the new position is. However, later adoptions usually indicate that there have been so many other traumas and so much pain in the child's life that the birth order characteristics may be very distorted.

f. DISABILITIES

The usual result of a disability in a child is to make that child the functional youngest — babied, protected, dependent — no matter what the birth order position is. This is particularly noticeable if the parents react as though the disability is an insurmountable obstacle or a tragedy. Even when the disability is relatively minor — such as loss of the use of an arm — such a child is likely to be an underfunctioner and not perform according to normal birth order characteristics.

On the other hand, if the parents have a more positive attitude and treat the child like any other child, expecting him or her to deal with the disability, the child is better able to overcome it and more likely to develop the personality traits of any other child in that birth order position. Middle child Stevie Wonder seems to enjoy the attention he gets as a performer without being hampered by his blindness.

If a sibling is severely disabled or chronically ill, the next one in line usually fills in that sibling position role, but with fewer emotional complications than when a sibling has died. This is most evident when it is the oldest or an older middle who is disabled and when the disability has existed from birth. Lawrence, a middle child by birth order, is functionally an oldest because his older brother, Darren, has Down's Syndrome and has never been able to function as an oldest. Lawrence's younger sister, Micheline, is functionally like a middle child because Darren acts like and is treated like a youngest.

The disability of a sibling often causes more difficulties for sisters than brothers because the female child is expected to do more of the caretaking. A youngest sister may become like an oldest because of family expectations that she take more responsibility for a disabled sibling, while her older brother may still have a relatively carefree life.

g. ANXIETY IN THE FAMILY

A child born during a time of great stress in the family may have characteristics that deviate from most other people in the same birth order position. When the family is not functioning normally, the usual patterns of development are interrupted. A parent who ordinarily might have been very nurturing might become neglectful of a child during a time of anxiety, and the expected personality development of that child will be altered.

The cause of the anxiety may be external, such as a war or economic depression that affects the entire population, or internal, such as the loss of a job or the temporary illness of a family member.

Another kind of anxiety is related to repeating a pattern of emotional dynamics over a few generations in the family. Professionals call this the "family projection process." One way it happens is when a child becomes the intense emotional focus of one or both parents. Children in this situation will not go through the same pattern of development as others in their birth order position.

This process happens frequently when feelings and perceptions are transferred from the generation before the parent to the generation following. A child in that case becomes the recipient of emotions derived from a parent's relationship with the child's grandparents, not with the child.

Rowena was the oldest of five children and her mother (a youngest) relied on her a great deal to help run the family, fix meals, look after the kids, and basically keep things organized. When Rowena married and became the mother of a daughter, Juliana, she vowed not to burden Juliana the way her mother had burdened her. Her next child was a son, and then she had two more daughters. Juliana was not allowed, let alone encouraged, to do any of the typical oldest child activities in the family. Rowena meant to spare Juliana and give her the kind of childhood she wished for herself. But, as a result of this reaction, Juliana became a severely underfunctioning woman who remained dependent on others, including her mother and siblings, for the rest of her life. Juliana did not develop any of the typical oldest sister traits because her mother projected her own past experience onto Juliana's present.

This process can occur whether the qualities projected onto the child are positive or negative. It can be just as damaging to be marked as the "good" person; the artificial designation still inhibits natural development.

Evan's grandmother died when his mother Zelda was an infant, so Zelda never knew her mother, but was always told that her mother was a "saint" and "a devoted Catholic." Zelda loved this mother she had never met and kept a picture of her on her dresser all of her adult life, even though her own life was much more freewheeling and revolved around going drinking rather than going to church. Zelda had Evan out of wedlock and lived most of her parenting years as a single mother. But she found herself raising a "good" son. She had trouble ever identifying any "bad" qualities in him and was sometimes a little put off by his self-righteousness. She never voiced any comparisons between her mother and her son, and she may never have consciously made the connection, but Evan, without hesitation and without consulting her, decided to become a priest.

While Evan never experienced any overtly negative results from this projection process, he eventually found that he was so concerned about appearing to be "right" and "good" and getting other people's approval that he wasn't able to be himself. He was so busy being his saintly grandmother that he wasn't doing or saying what made sense to him and what he believed and felt. It took him a number of years to learn to be honest first with himself and then with the important people in his life, including his mother.

Single parent Lorna began having trouble with her 17-year-old son, Jack, the oldest of two boys. She thought he was becoming "just like his father" and like her own father, both of whom she detested. She complained about Jack's willfulness and desire to have things his own way. She had always been attracted to "strong" men and her fantasy had been that they would use their strength to take care of her. Instead, they used it to get their way with her, from her point of view, and she felt unable to cope with that strength.

In many ways, Jack was just acting like a normal older brother of a brother, but her fear that he was becoming like his father intensified what would have been the expected disagreements between a teenager and parent. The more she tried to squelch his take-charge style, the angrier Jack became and the more energy he put into resisting her and, to some extent, playing out the role her father had had in relation to her. At one point, Jack actually hit her during an argument. Jack's development as a competent, responsible oldest was sidetracked, and instead he became a competent, rebellious child who did well at being bad and eventually became the leader of a drug ring in his high school.

The oldest child and the youngest child in the family are particularly vulnerable to being focused on in ways that change the usual development patterns for their birth order.

Erika, an unmarried woman in her mid-30s, sought therapy because she was having trouble allowing herself to become close to men. She was the youngest of five brothers and sisters. She had left her native Germany and moved to Canada specifically to get away from her family. However, she felt guilty about leaving, as though she had abandoned her mother. Although physically distant, she was still tied emotionally to her family and was unable to allow herself to "betray" mother and make a commitment to a husband and family of her own.

During the course of therapy, it became clear that at her birth, her mother had figuratively said to herself, "This one is for my old age." She expected Erika to be the one to stay home and take care of her, rather than go off to get married. Although never articulated, this goal permeated Erika's childhood in such a way that she developed few of the characteristics of a youngest sister of brothers. She was weighed down by her sense of responsibility to her mother, and in many ways seemed like an oldest child.

Sometimes the special focus on a child comes as a result of unwanted pregnancies, premature births, and adoptions. Each of these events can create stress in the family and lead to changes in the behavior of parents and siblings that affect the usual development of the child.

Marie-Lou, a Roman Catholic, had not wanted to have children but did so out of duty and was a reasonably nurturing parent to her four children. Then, 12 years after her last child was born and just as she was beginning to feel as though her life was her own, Marie-Lou became pregnant again. Her anger about this was focused on the child, who had a difficult time growing up and was often deeply depressed and suicidal, unlike most youngests.

A child can also become the unnatural focus of the family when the parents have a conflictual relationship, whether or not they actually divorce. The oldest child, who may be the one most aware of the tension in the house or the one who bears the brunt of the parents' bitterness, can become weak and whining, and the next oldest child will take on the characteristics of an oldest child, becoming more responsible or trying to take care of the oldest. Another result is that the oldest child will become like a rebellious youngest. Researcher Frank Sulloway found that strong parental conflict, most frequently in lower-class families, led some oldest-child scientists to become the radical thinkers unlike the usual more conventional oldest children. Isaac Newton is one example of an oldest who had a disruptive childhood and started a scientific revolution.

h. LARGE FAMILIES

Birth order characteristics in very large families (eight or more children) tend to become confused or diluted. So many sub-groups can form that there may be several "oldests" and several "youngests" who are actually middles. Or the first two may both be like oldests and the last two like youngests, with all the rest like middles. Sometimes the oldest and the youngest pair off in an affectionate, parent-child kind of relationship, which distorts the birth order characteristics of those around them.

Very large families often have less money than other families, so the children have fewer "nice" things and the parents must struggle to make ends meet. The stress of this situation — combined with the limited attention the parents are able to give each child — can increase the normal sibling jealousy and create bitterness among the children as they are forced to share the scanty resources.

16
PARENTING YOUR CHILDREN OF DIFFERENT BIRTH ORDERS

There are only two lasting bequests we can hope to give our children. One of these is roots; the other, wings.

Hodding Carter

Siblings develop not only in relation to each other but also in re-action to how their parents treat them (or are perceived to treat them) in relation to each other. What follows are some general guidelines for parenting in relation to sibling issues. These supplement the suggestions to parents provided at the end of each particular birth order section.

...I could hear my father talking to my mother Mama asked: "Which of the two do you like best?" [He said,] "Simone is more serious-minded, but Poupette is so affectionate." They went on weighing the pros and the cons of our case, speaking their inmost thoughts quite

freely; finally they agreed that they loved us both equally well: it was just like what you read in books about wise parents whose love is the same for all their children.

Simone de Beauvoir,
Memoirs of a Dutiful Daughter

Most parents today have been sensitized to the fact that they should love each child equally and not play favorites, but there are many other ways that you as a parent can contribute positively to the sibling relationships between your children and, therefore, the life success of each child.

a. DEALING WITH JEALOUSY

As you are probably well aware, babies come into the world thinking that they are the world. They want it all, and they want it right now, as their crying graphically demonstrates at all hours of the night. This changes only slowly as they learn what concessions they must make to be accepted at home and in the world and how they must behave to get at least some of what they want.

Within the family, each child (maybe even each adult) wants to be loved the most. For each child, the birth of a new child is a loss rather than a gain. Children do not naturally want to share your love and attention with the person they see as a usurper. First children especially have no reason to love a new baby, someone they don't even know. Yet siblings are expected to like, even love, one another.

This causes inner turmoil because the older children know they are supposed to be happy about the new arrival, but they are not. If they express their unhappiness, their parents are unhappy with them. This is the way most sibling relationships begin, and the flavor of this first experience can last long into adulthood for the siblings.

Florence Nightingale was often unhappy and fretted over her relationship with her older sister who apparently was jealous of Florence's attractiveness and wit. According to the biography *Florence Nightingale,* she wrote to her sister at the age of 10, "Let us love each other better than we have done. It is the will of God and Mamma particularly desires it."

On the other hand, some children deal with the jealousy by identifying with their parents and becoming a second parent to the new baby. In this way they try to keep a connection with mother. This can easily begin a lifetime pattern of caretaking for the older child. He or she may grow up too fast and, rather than doing a good job of taking care of himself or herself, learn to take care of others. As an adult, this person may be an over-functioner who always takes care of others.

The younger sibling of an overfunctioner may become very dependent on this caretaking and become an underfunctioner, never developing all of his or her skills.

Expecting your children to provide nurture and support for each other is imposing an unrealistic burden on the children. Children simply do not have the inner resources to do this and attempting it can put them in conflict with their own developmental needs. Childhood is a time for being taken care of, not being a caretaker. It is not unusual to find that some oldest children deeply resented having the responsibility of taking care of their younger siblings imposed on them by their parents. Some oldests even decide, as adults, not to have children of their own; they feel they have already raised a family.

Accept that your children will not *want* to share with their siblings. It is natural that they will not want to share their toys — or anything else — so don't make them share everything. Respect each child's need to have private property that is off limits to the others. Don't expect more generosity or kindness than a child is able to give. Generosity is a learned response, not a natural instinct, and it doesn't come easily. Think of how willing you would be to share all your possessions with a neighbor or friend, especially if you see that person not taking good care of your things.

Recognize that each birth order position presents special difficulties. A child's negative reactions to events in the family may be justified in many cases. It's not easy to be the oldest and told you have to babysit for the youngest when you would rather do something with your friends. It's not easy to be the youngest and told to keep your hands off your brother's toys. As a parent, you don't have to fix all the problems associated with sibling rivalry, but you can listen to the complaints of each child. Whether or not you agree that the complaint is justified, show that you understand and sympathize. Do not disparage the child's feelings, just hear him or her out and reassure the unhappy child that you accept him or her, and believe they can work things out.

b. DISCOURAGING COMPETITIVENESS

Children with siblings can begin to believe that they have to be the best to be loved the most. They don't think they have to be best in the world necessarily, just best among the current contenders — the other kids in the house.

There is enough competitiveness out in the world — in the classroom, the playground, the sports field, the dance class — without children having to compete with each other at home. The family is supposed to be the place where you are loved for you, not for your accomplishments or abilities. Giving out gold stars and keeping charts of performance is a way of measuring and comparing the children that implies they are not lovable if they don't measure up.

Each child may believe that the others in the family are better loved and treated better. This is usually (though not always) a matter of their misperception, but comparing them to each other or praising one at the expense of another only reinforces such misperceptions. And most children (and adults) are already painfully aware of their shortcomings; they don't need to be reminded of them too often.

Your children will compete no matter what you do. You can't eliminate it, but you can modify the competition and make it more benign. One way, for example, is to be sure that when the family plays competitive games, losing is as acceptable and respectable as winning. Losing should not mean that your child is a loser. Being loved should not be associated with winning.

c. ACCEPTING THE DIFFERENCES AMONG YOUR CHILDREN

As the birth order descriptions make clear, there are abundant differences among the children in a family just by virtue of their birth order and gender, not to mention their genetic makeup and environmental influences. You can help make these differences a source of pride rather than regret by the way you treat each of your children.

In the first place, recognize that even a year's difference in age between siblings puts them on very different developmental scales. Don't expect the younger child to be as skilled at any task or as mature in any way as the older child. In fact, since oldest children are usually old beyond their years because of their accelerated development while they were the only child, you can expect your younger child to be more immature than the oldest was at the same age.

As children grow up, they figure out who they are and develop their identities by figuring out who the others in the family are. Each child wants to be unique and accepted as an individual. To be distinctive, a younger sibling usually does not try to compete in the same arena as an older sibling. The chances of successfully outshining the older child are slim. Instead, the second child will make a point of developing different skills, interests, and habits.

Parents who either say out loud, or silently wish, that one sibling (usually a younger one) was more like the other, fail to understand this important principle. The last thing these children want to do is be like each other. For the sake of healthy development in your children, you need to find ways to appreciate and affirm the differences between them. Notice the strengths and abilities that each child brings and affirm these, clearly and verbally: "You are good at ...."

Enjoy the variety in your family. Appreciate the individuality of each child and emphasize that most things are not good or bad in themselves. Having curly hair or straight hair, being tall or short, having blue eyes or black eyes shouldn't be a matter of pride or regret. The mother who laments that her daughter doesn't have curly hair like her son is being unfair to both.

If you hold up your older child as "the good, obedient one" whom the younger one should emulate, you run the risk that the more the older one tries to stand out by being good, the more the younger one will try to stand out by being "bad." Even though this will not be in the best interests of the younger child, it will feel better to the child than simply being an unsuccessful clone of the older sibling. Being a clone would mean being indistinguishable and, therefore, nonexistent — a nobody. Each child wants to be accepted for his or her own uniqueness, and this is what you must watch for and praise.

This is more difficult than it sounds when one sibling (usually the oldest) emulates your beliefs and values. You can't help but feel validated by this and like the child better for it. For example, well-educated parents are usually proud of an oldest who is a good student, and they do their best to encourage it. However, the second child of the same sex will rarely display the same serious interest and academic ability since that territory has already been claimed by the older one. That younger sibling's attempts to be different by being more social and outgoing may be seen by the parents as being frivolous and irresponsible. If the younger sibling is more interested in sports than in books, the parents may be disappointed and even embarrassed.

Trying to make a younger child into a smaller version of an older child is demeaning to both children and usually futile as well. The older child doesn't want the competition either, and if you succeed in pushing the younger child in that direction, the older child is likely to become more hostile and try to subvert the younger's efforts.

The reverse can also happen, of course. If the parents are youngests and didn't share the academic interests of their older siblings, they may fail to support their more introverted, serious oldest child.

Another common scenario is when the oldest child starts to go through the normal rebellious stage of teenagehood and the parents can't accept it and react frantically. Then their attitudes change; they think their older child is difficult and their younger, still obedient, child becomes the "good" one. Of course, comparing a teenager to a nine-year-old is like comparing a Harley Davidson to a tricycle, but many parents make that comparison and label the children accordingly.

The key is learning to feel comfortable with each child's "differentness" and finding positive things in that to appreciate and support. Don't compare the children. Value each child as is. Attempting to enforce sameness among your children is likely to create either significant rebellion or overtly obedient but inwardly demoralized and depressed children.

If you are comfortable with, and can appreciate, differences in other areas of your life — say between you and your spouse — you will be better able to be more supportive of the differences between your children. A family that can affirm the differences between family members is a more cohesive one than the one that tends to expect just one way of being in the world. When differences are unacceptable, children in those families often decide that the only way they can exist as a separate self is to get away from their family.

Another way children in these families react is to become so fearful of losing even the tenuous approval of their parents that they give up their own identity, become what the parents want them to be, and end up dependent and depressed for the rest of their lives.

d. DON'T ASSIGN ROLES

Even if you manage to accept the differences in your children, you are still not out of the woods. You can fall into the trap of enforcing those differences to the point of assigning lifetime roles to the children: the quiet one, the brave one, the witty one or, more harmfully, the nervous one, the ineffectual one, the crazy one. Children are always in the process of creating themselves and easily identify with roles that are ascribed to them. Told often enough that they are clumsy or agile, stupid or smart, plain or beautiful, they begin to think that is how they are, and that severely limits their options for what they become.

Part of accepting the differences among your children is accepting the differences within each child. A child can easily be clumsy at different stages of growth and development, but it doesn't mean you have a clumsy child, as long as you allow for different behavior to emerge by not labeling the child. The witty child may not have anything funny to say some days and shouldn't be pressured to live up to some image of the comedian in order to be accepted or noticed.

Clara came into therapy with her husband when she was in her late thirties. They did not have severe marital problems, but she felt depressed and "restricted" in her life. He was concerned that he was "causing" this in some way, but Clara couldn't identify anything specific in her husband's behavior that would cause it.

She was the youngest of three sisters. All three of the women had successfully pursued careers, as well as getting married and having children. Clara had started her own business, which was profitable, but she was seen by others in the family and by herself as the least successful of the three sisters. When she talked about the messages she had gotten from her parents as a child, she said that her mother in particular had been quite good about not expecting the girls to be the same. They were each told that they were different and had their own gifts and ways of being special and that mom loved them all.

But as Clara continued to look at this issue she began to identify the source of her discomfort. In stressing their different attributes, mom had given roles to each of the girls: the oldest had a practical head, was well organized, responsible, and got things done; the middle girl was good with figures and abstract theories; and Clara was told that she was mom's "artistic and spiritual" daughter. As a child, Clara liked hearing mom tell her what she was good at, and she identified with these ascribed roles and worked hard at getting affirmation through them. But as an adult she had begun to find her image limiting and restrictive. Therapy involved her beginning to claim more of the skills and abilities that she had denied in herself for many years, including being practical and well organized and having a good head for business.

When each new child is born into the family, the other members of the family have already developed their own identities and roles. These roles tend to require complementary roles and identities to achieve a sense of emotional balance in the family.

The more emotionally stuck together the family is, the stronger the need to create complementary roles and identities. When this need is not met, there is a buildup of anxiety in the family, which children are very responsive to. This kind of anxiety creates a tremendous sense of insecurity, which children will try to avoid at any cost. They will give up themselves in order to lower the sense of anxiety, both in themselves and in other important figures — especially their parents.

If the family is able to allow each child to develop his or her own identity without reference to what others expect, the range of options for personal development is greater. The more the child senses that the identity of the parents and siblings is not threatened by his or her own developing identity, the greater freedom the child has to develop in unique and truly individual directions, while still being able to maintain a close connection with family members.

Being in close connection while being an individual is the critical element. A lot of people are able to nurture their "individuality" by keeping distant from their families. Indeed, they believe that to stay away from family is the only way to maintain their sense of self. All contact with the family is seen as leading to a loss of self. When children feel forced to flee from the family in this way, their sense of identity is actually very fragile. Their emotional distancing is motivated by their doubts about being able to be themselves in the family context and later in other intimate relationships like marriage.

The individuality they have developed and prized within themselves may be a pseudo-individuality. It was an identity they developed to fill a void in the family. The family for some reason may have needed a rebellious or apparently unique character who insisted on doing things "his way" in order to balance out other members in the family. This "individuality" is then not a freely chosen expression of self, but a fulfillment of a family need to have such a character.

As adults, these children will be compelled to seek out people who will play the same role as family members did in order for them to feel comfortable in their role.

For example, a child who reacts against a rigid, dogmatically religious family often ends up involved in the same kind of situation outside the family. It may not be a religious group, but might be some other kind of rigidly structured group that tries to enforce sameness among its members — a motorcycle gang, a cell of revolutionaries, a commune of elitist artists, or a political party of neo-fascists. The adult then reacts against the expectations and restrictions of that group the way the child did against the parents.

This caution about not assigning roles applies to birth order roles also. Though this book may help you understand your children's behavior better given their birth order positions, you should not use this knowledge to pigeon-hole any of the children. Remember, the descriptions merely describe the likely effects of birth order, not what anyone must be or should be like.

If anything, being aware of the self-limiting function of birth order roles should enable you to help your children broaden their horizons by reaching beyond the conventional limitations of their birth order position.

e. PROVIDING EQUAL OPPORTUNITIES

One of the differences among siblings that has been ritually accepted and promoted to excess is that of gender. As mentioned earlier, almost without exception parents and everyone else treat girl children differently from boy children. Sex discrimination begins in the home, and the place where it can be most effectively ended is in the home.

Elizabeth Cady Stanton, 19th century feminist, said this about her only brother's death when she was 11: "I still recall my father seated by his side...thinking of the wreck of all his hopes in the loss of a dear son He took no notice of me. I resolved I would study and strive to be at the head of all my classes and thus delight my father's heart." She won a prize in Greek and thought that would make her father "satisfied" with her. "He kissed me on the forehead and exclaimed, with a sigh, `Ah, you should have been a boy!' My joy was turned to ashes."

This kind of reaction on the part of even a loving parent still happens today. While there are bona fide differences in the way males and females develop and the way they relate to the world, these differences ought not to be the basis of deciding what one child will be allowed to do and another not allowed to do.

A youngest daughter whose parents believe she has as many abilities as her older brother and is worth "investing in" receives a significant gift from her parents. She will be allowed to explore the full range of options in the same way her brother might.

A daughter who is not overprotected, but encouraged to try the same "risky" activities as a boy might well grow up less fearful and more sure of herself than a daughter who is considered too delicate or too ladylike for rough play.

Women from all-girl families, particularly oldest sisters, are statistically much higher achievers and more successful in their careers than women from mixed sibling families, which seems to indicate that when a male is in the family, less encouragement is given to the females.

Boys, too, need to be given more options for their life roles. Parents can do this, for instance, by giving their sons equal responsibility for doing household chores (inside the house, not just mowing the lawn) and for taking care of younger siblings (rather than leaving it all to their sisters) and teaching them the language of feelings and helping them to acknowledge these feelings within themselves.

The important thing is not to restrict any child from certain spheres of endeavor because of their sex or any other reason.

Of course, as in most things that parents attempt to teach their children, the most effective teaching is by example. The parents' own way of relating as male and female and of functioning as a competent woman and a nurturing man will have the greatest impact on the gender role development of the children. One of the things to consider in choosing a future spouse might be whether that is the kind of man or woman you want your son or your daughter to be like when grown.

f.   DON'T TREAT THEM IDENTICALLY

Treating your children as equals does not mean treating them all the same. Since your children are different from each other, it's logical that what they need from you varies from one to the other. Trying to treat them all exactly the same is difficult and frustrating as well as being self-defeating. Rather than trying to equally divide yourself between them and duplicating your every encounter, respond to them individually according to the tastes and needs of each one. Your middle child, for example, may need and appreciate your undivided attention right now much more than your oldest, who may need less attention at this stage of life and want more freedom.

Don't assume that all the children should have all the same experiences. Don't automatically send all the children to the same camp or the same recreation center. Offer them the option of finding a new place to go that might be a better fit for them.

They may not even want the same gifts at the same age. Just because Concetta liked getting roller skates at age five, it doesn't necessarily follow that Margarita will too. The best way to find out is to leave it open-ended by asking not "Do you want skates like Concetta got?" but "What would you like?"

Many families are proud of their "initiation" rituals, where at a certain age they present each child with a symbol of having passed the milestone. For example, "We give all the girls a lipstick and a pair of pantyhose at age 12." That may be okay as a ritual as long as you don't expect them all to be equally grateful or interested in using those things. Your middle daughter, for example, may not be interested in wearing lipstick until she's 15, but would dearly love to get a hockey stick. But then, as the section above warns, don't lock her into being "the athlete" when she may decide she wants a frilly dress the next year. Offering options and accepting choices is one of the most loving things parents can do.

Help your children learn to make decisions for themselves on the basis of their own values and needs rather than yours or their siblings. Try to give them options as often as is feasible. If you go out for dinner, ask what they want — whether it's a hamburger or a hot dog or fettucine. Don't give hints about what *you* want them to want. If you absolutely don't want them to have something, don't offer it as a choice. If you offer a choice, don't undermine it by disapproving of their decision. Don't, under any circumstances, say "Why don't you get what your sister got?"

To find out more about each child's individual needs, make it a point to spend some time alone with each child during a week. It doesn't have to be, and shouldn't be, the same amount of time with each child each week, but according to your schedule and their needs. You might spend some of this time together while you are doing other chores or errands, but be sure you are not using it as a chance to teach the child or get some work out of your child. Let the time be focused on finding out about your child's wants and needs.

In the interests of fairness and reducing resentment, you may need to set the same boundaries for each child according to age, but the way you enforce them may vary according to each child. For instance, you may have the same midnight curfew for each child who turns 16, but being kept in for a week might be more effective enforcement for one, while no television for a week is more persuasive for another.

g. PARENTING OUT OF YOUR OWN BIRTH ORDER

Another way to make use of the concepts in this book is to be aware of the different strengths and liabilities you bring from your own sibling position to the parenting role. As indicated in chapter 2 and in the birth order descriptions, each sibling position has its own unique gifts for this job, and its deficits and blank spots.

Parents who are in different sibling positions themselves can complement each other in their parenting roles or they can clash in such a way that they are unable to parent as a team in a mutually supportive way.

Nick was a second oldest brother. His father was also the second male in his family and his mother was the oldest child in her family. Verbally and overtly both parents held up the oldest son as the model to be followed by the other two siblings (the youngest was a daughter). But Nick's father covertly sent messages to Nick that he really liked Nick's more rebellious style. For example, he would laugh heartily at stories of Nick's escapades and repeat them to his buddies. But since mom and dad could not openly acknowledge their different beliefs about bringing up children, they both said they wanted Nick to be more responsible, but Nick was confused by the mixed messages and became a mixed-up kid.

This confusion was evident in the way he behaved in his own marriage, and especially in the way he parented his two boys. He found himself sending conflicting messages to them and doing to them what his father had done to him in overtly praising the behavior of the oldest, but covertly admiring the rambunctious younger son.

Clarifying the role of sibling issues in his own family helped Nick to be clearer about his goals in his marriage, as a parent, and also in the way he ran his own business, where his employees were often confused about just what he wanted from them.

An oldest sibling parent and a youngest sibling parent may be able to bring the best of both worlds to their kids in their modeling of behavior, especially if their children have the same birth order. Or that combination may constantly fight over the best way to raise kids and the kinds of values they want to instill in their children. The oldest sibling parent may want the children to have high standards of performance and get to the top of their careers, while the youngest sibling parent just wants them to enjoy life and take it easy.

On the other hand, children raised by parents who are both oldests or both youngests may get an overdose of one particular style of parenting and have to work all the harder to create their own unique way of being in the world.

Jean-Paul and Teresa were both oldest children married to each other. Jean-Paul was, in fact, an oldest brother of an oldest brother of an oldest brother. Not surprisingly Jean-Paul and Teresa's oldest son excelled in high school and was "a model son." Also not surprisingly, their second son Victor (two years younger) was "just the opposite" and was a constant problem and source of frustration for them. Victor said he felt "totally misunderstood" and "unsupported" in the family, and he was sure he was not their child.

It took much hard work for Jean-Paul and Teresa to begin to accept that not all children can or should be like an oldest child and to appreciate Victor's special younger child traits. A major resource for them in working on this problem was their own siblings, with whom they had had rather distant and ritualized relationships previously. Jean-Paul and Teresa made a point of asking their brothers and sisters about the experience of growing up with them as the "good" oldest child. Their siblings helped them see the pain of growing up being compared to someone whom they could never measure up to. Eventually they became more appreciative of their second son, but it took several more years for this changed stance to have a positive impact on Victor.

h. DIVORCED PARENTS

As mentioned in chapter 15, divorce can affect children to such a degree that they end up with characteristics other than what are usual for their birth order. When the parents continue their battles after separating, the siblings sometimes replay those battles among themselves, taking sides and blaming each other for their parents' problems.

You have to be careful to impress your children with the fact that the problems between you and your spouse are adult problems that have nothing to do with them. It is destructive for you and the children to try to turn them against their other parent, no matter how hurt and angry you are at your spouse. It's your battle, and your children have a right to develop their own relationship with each parent. They will not necessarily develop the same kind of negative relationship the two of you developed. And remember that you were once attracted to that person, so there must be some redeeming quality there that your children can relate to.

Even if you and your spouse are conscientious about having the children regularly visit the noncustodial parent, your children may still be struggling with feelings of abandonment and insecurity. Watch for changes in their behavior and departures from the standard reactions for their birth order position. Help them to express their feelings and need for reassurance in ways that are socially acceptable rather than anti-social. It may simply mean that you need to play more games with your youngest or talk more with your oldest.

i. YOUR CHILDREN ARE NOT YOUR SIBLINGS

The way parents perceive the sibling relationship of their children is often determined by their own experience of sibling relationships in their family of origin. You need to be aware that some of your reactions to your children's relationship with each other may come out of your history with your siblings. Frequently, even before the birth of the children, parents fantasize about a vision of their "ideal family" and just how they want their children to relate to each other. This fantasy is almost always based on their own experience in their family of origin; either they want to replicate the good experience they had in their own families or they want to improve upon or do the opposite of what they experienced in their families. Because these expectations are separate from the reality of who their children are, they can become a frustrating experience for everyone involved.

Ingrid brought her three daughters to family therapy because they fought with each other so often. She could not stand their fighting and would continually break them up and lecture them on the need to "love one another" as sisters. If this failed, she became so uncomfortable she would leave the house. The background of this sensitivity was the truly violent fights that happened between her and her two sisters while they were growing up. She was never able to let her daughters work out their own relationship because of her fear that the anger would be physically expressed, which it never had been.

Gaining some insight into your own development can be accomplished by asking your parents in a friendly and interested way about their experiences in their own families of origin and how those experiences shaped their intentions and actions in the family they created. What kind of hopes and visions did they have for their children even before they were born? What was the basis of these hopes? How did they try to bring about the realization of these hopes? How well do they think it worked? What might they now do differently in their own families of origin?

Also think back to your childhood relationship with your siblings. Is there anything familiar about your relationship now with one or more of your children? A parent's relationship with a sibling is often unknowingly transferred to the relationship with a child. It's not at all unusual for a person in therapy who is researching the background of the hostility between him or her and a parent to discover that the parent had a similarly hostile or difficult relationship with a sibling. The child may have been told, "You are just like your Aunt So and So," but often no one realizes that the parent is continually reacting to the old sibling issues.

Genevieve brought her two sons in for family therapy because of problems she was having with her younger son. When asked at some point who he reminded her of, Genevieve realized he seemed much like her younger brother as a child, the family black sheep. She had great contempt for her brother, which was coloring the way she saw her son. The therapist first asked her to identify the many ways her son was different from her brother. Then Genevieve was given the task of getting to know her brother better and in a new way. After a few false starts, she developed a less hostile relationship with her brother, and her attitude toward her son also changed for the better.

* * *

Finally, you might keep in mind these words by Anne Frank, written in *The Diary of a Young Girl*: "[Daddy] said: `All children must look after their own upbringing.' Parents can only give good advice or put them on the right paths, but the final forming of a person's character lies in their own hands."

17
SIBLINGS AS A PSYCHOLOGICAL RESOURCE

Falling leaves settle to their roots.

Chinese proverb

The death of our last parent heightens our awareness of mortality. Our sense of aloneness in the universe becomes more acute, and our own death seems more imminent. An ongoing connection with brothers and sisters helps keep this feeling at bay or alleviate its intensity. The need to be known by someone consistently over all the years of life — through different moves and major changes — can best be met by siblings.

A long-term, stable marriage meets some of this need, but as more people stay single and nearly half of all marriages end in divorce, this option is becoming less likely. And anyway, even in the best case, your spouse has not known you for as long and in some ways as intimately as your siblings have.

The thread of historical continuity provided in the sibling connection can be a tremendous source of support as people struggle with the emotional challenges of life — suffering through the pain and rejoicing in the victories. In the middle and later years of adult life, nothing else can compare with what siblings have to offer each other, even if they are not particularly close and rarely spend any time together. Your siblings are the people who know the most about you and your roots.

Recently, researchers have found that the emotional health of men at age 65 is strongly connected to having had a close relationship with their siblings at college age. This study of Harvard graduates (males) has been ongoing since the early 1940s when psychiatrist George Vaillant started interviewing the men every five years. In their middle years, a good marriage and good job were the most important variables, but by retirement their earlier relationship with siblings was deemed far more important to their well-being.

The field of psychotherapy and of human psychology generally has paid a great deal of attention to the ongoing relationship of parents and adult children, but has paid scant attention to the sibling connection. Some family therapists today are becoming increasingly aware of the importance of this relationship. Clients are encouraged to contact siblings they have lost touch with, to raise new kinds of questions with those they do have contact with, and to invite their siblings to their therapy sessions. This is always a powerful experience, full of new illuminations and insights.

One of the most exciting parts of personal growth and change is being able to reconnect with your family members in a new way, a way that shows interest in how they experienced life in the family. This is a change from being concerned solely with your own experiences and trying to convince others that your interpretation of "the way it really was" is the correct one.

Each member of a family puts the pieces of the family puzzle together differently, which creates several different pictures. Whenever a family member insists that his or her picture is the "right" one, relationships within the family suffer. Family members commonly diagnose what they believe to be the strengths and liabilities of their family, but the more adamant they are about the diagnosis, the less able they are to grow and change. Every time you set another family member into concrete with a label such as "saintly," "rigid," "domineering," "compliant," "alcoholic," "cute," "mean," "wonderful," etc., you also make more rigid your view of yourself. To say someone else is "always like this" is to say something similar about yourself. It means that you only see that one aspect of them and treat them as if they have no other characteristics.

Just as you may think you have other family members figured out, they also may think they have you figured out. But, in fact, family members are often strangers to each other. You may deduce a lot from observing each other's behavior, but without knowing another person from the inside, you can never be sure about them.

Even though you and your siblings have lived through many of the same events, you each experienced them differently, and that different experience is part of what contributed to making you different people, which leads you to experience and interpret things differently — and so on. Your siblings' different interpretation of family and events can be invaluable to you in your attempts to make sense of your life. Your siblings can help you recall events and comments that you had long forgotten or blocked out, but that may have been extremely significant in shaping your experience. They can remind you of capabilities and gifts you had as a child, which they admired, that you may have lost touch with over the years.

Even your siblings' criticism of you, if you can hear it non-defensively, is a gift of learning about yourself. Even when the criticism is inaccurate, it gives you another way of thinking about how you got to be the person you are.

Most people do not think of using their siblings as a psychological or emotional resource for personal growth. If they turn to their brothers and sisters at all, it may only be during times of family crisis or significant stress. This is fine; it is another kind of support siblings have to offer each other. It is not uncommon to see men in their fifties, without a single intimate friend they can confide in, turn to a (usually older) sister for help in times of trouble. Being there at the crisis times is a tremendous service siblings provide each other.

...[when] one looks back at childhood, the only truth is what you remember. No one else who was there can agree with you because he has his own version of what he saw. He also holds to a personal truth of himself, based on an indefatigable self-regard. One neighbor's reaction, after reading my [autobiography], sums up this double vision. "You hit off old Tom to the life," he said. "But why d'you tell all those lies about me?"

Seven brothers and sisters shared my early years, and we lived on top of each other. If they all had written of those days, each account would have been different, and each one true. We saw the same events at different heights, at different levels of mood and hunger — one suppressing an incident as too much to bear, another building it large around him, each reflecting one world according to the temper of his day, his age, the chance heat of his blood. Recalling it differently, as we were bound to do, what was it, in fact, we saw? Which one among us has the truth of it now? And which one shall be the judge? The truth is, of course, that there is no pure truth, only the moody accounts of witnesses.

Laurie Lee, *I Can't Stay Long*

It is even more rewarding, however, to establish the kind of relationship where, in calmer and less stressful times, you can together reflect on your experience of growing up — how it varied for each of you, how you each developed in your own unique ways, how you went your different directions.

Phil Donahue reports in his autobiography that because of the five-year age difference between him and his sister, they had little to do with each other as children. "It was much later," he writes, "when we were both well into adulthood, that I came to really know my sister. Today we share a close and caring friendship."

If that kind of relationship doesn't develop naturally, you can cultivate it intentionally. Three adult brothers decided that they wanted to put behind them some of the problems that had developed among them over the years. Together, they sought the help of a family therapist. As oldest, middle, and youngest brothers, they closely matched the sibling position characteristics described in this book. Those characteristics, and how they came about as a result of their positions in the family, had been part of the reason for their divisions and emotional distance from each other over the years. Their characteristics were also the reason each had been able to put together a satisfying life according to their own style and values.

They had run into trouble in their relationship when one brother tried to insist that the others see things and do things his way, or when two of them ganged up on the third to tell him he was "wrong." What they needed to understand was that it was normal for them to have such different ways of approaching life and that those differences did not have to be a detriment to their relationship.

They began to learn to use their different perspectives to help each other think through their own positions and values, rather than demanding that the others think or feel the same way. They discovered that their differences could be a rich resource and that they did not have to become like each other to have a good relationship. They could each develop individually while also being connected to one another.

This revelation about their sibling relationship also helped them in other relationships where they had developed similar and unsatisfying ways of relating. For example, Earl, the oldest brother, was often upset and impatient with his two youngest children. He took the risk of sharing his frustration with his brothers. They told him what it had been like for them to be on the receiving end of his impatience as children — how hurt they had felt by his criticism. The middle brother spoke with tears in his eyes about how he had tried to impress Earl, only to have Earl say it wasn't good enough and make his achievements look insignificant. Earl was able to trace back the origin of his impatience with his brothers to the high expectations their father had of him. Their father had emphasized that it was Earl's job to make sure the younger boys did well. It was news to the two brothers that when they made mistakes Earl was punished. Earl could see that he had the same anxiety about his younger children performing perfectly, even though he was the father in charge now.

The siblings who relate comfortably with each other as adults are those who have been able to find some way to affirm themselves in the context of their sibling relationship. If their closeness or connection with each other did not happen at the expense of their separate identities, they can have a fairly happy relationship. For example, oldest siblings who felt comfortable and good about themselves in taking care of a younger sibling were usually able to find something in it for themselves — a sense of autonomy or competence or knowledge. Youngests who felt affirmed by the attention of the oldest or learned some new skill that made the world an easier or more interesting place to live were able to appreciate the role of the oldest without resentment. Golda Meir, for example, wrote in her autobiography that her older sister was "a shining example, my dearest friend and my mentor."

However, problems develop when these roles become so rigid that neither sibling is able to develop an identity apart from the other. In that case, if the younger sibling suddenly stops listening to the older sibling, the older one may be frustrated and not know how to relate without being the one in charge. Or if the older sibling makes new friends as a teenager and loses interest in the younger sibling, the younger one may feel abandoned and left out. To the extent that the younger sibling's identity was based on getting attention from the older sibling, he or she will try to tag along — only to be rejected even more forcefully.

Siblings are rarely able to work these issues out with each other while they are young. But when they get older, beginning usually around the age of 30, they normally have enough sense of themselves that they can reconnect with each other in a new way. Then they can begin to learn from each other. Without doubt, the problems they had with each other are similar to the problems they have with others in their adult life. At this point, they may be mature enough to offer fresh perspectives on these issues to one another.

For there is no friend like a sister/In calm or stormy weather

Christina Rossetti, "Goblin Market"

Siblings need not become best friends or even part of each other's social circles. But even if there is contact only a few times a year, a good adult sibling relationship is money in the bank for those rainy days of emotional need. It enables you to draw on the perspective of an intimate "friend" who is different from you but "knows" you.

Not all sibling relationships are equally meaningful. Generally, the closer you are in age and the more years you spent living together in the same household, the more intense the relationship is. The intensity can be there whether or not you are in frequent, or even any, contact with your sibling. A cool, distant relationship that is the result of anger or hatred between siblings is just as intense emotionally as a warm, loving relationship. Siblings who have a great number of years between them or were perhaps raised separately by different parts of the family, have less intense, but often more benign, connections.

It is common today for siblings to lose touch with each other because they have moved to different parts of the country or the world. But physical distance does not end the emotional intensity of a relationship. Siblings can be apart from each other for 20 years and yet when they come back together again take up right where they left off emotionally.

When 76-year-old Marie was ill and near death, her 85-year-old sister, Jean, traveled 2,000 miles to come to the hospital bedside. Marie had not been eating and was very thin. Jean began to feed her from the hospital food tray. Unlike the doctors and nurses, and Marie's own children who spoke to her gently and tended to recognize her "right" not to eat, Jean leaned over the hospital bed and barked out commands in her raspy, quivery voice. "Open your mouth. Eat this. Chew. Swallow. Eat some more."

Marie compliantly ate a little, but finally rebelled and said in a voice that was barely audible but full of the emotional power of years of similar experiences, "You're so bossy." Immediately Jean replied, "And you're just as stubborn as you always were!"

This characteristic way of relating had spanned the lifetime of these two sisters. They had found ways during less stressful times to avoid getting into this typical childhood interaction. They had learned to become good supports for each other in spite of the geographical distance that separated them. But, as is normal in all emotional systems, when the level of anxiety goes up there is a tendency to revert to old patterns of behavior.

When people claim that their brothers and sisters are not important to them and they offer as proof the fact that they have not had any contact in many, many years, this is usually evidence of the power of the relationship. What is so important about this relationship that you have to keep so far away? What happens to your own sense of self when you are with this sibling? Keeping distance between you is often an attempt to avoid a powerful relationship, and this probably means you have some important unfinished issues to work on together. If you are able to do this work, it will most likely help you with other areas of your life as well.

One of the best ways you can use this chapter is to send copies of it to your siblings and suggest you get together to talk it over sometime soon. One psychiatrist who had seven brothers and sisters sent each of them a copy of Ron's book *Family Ties That Bind*. He asked them to make notes as they read the book and to mail these notes on to each other in a kind of round robin, so that everyone saw everyone else's notes. Then they spent a weekend together with a therapist and began to talk with each other about their experience in the family. It was not intended as an encounter session or a time of confrontation, but as a time of self-discovery for each individual. They all left the weekend saying it had been one of the most meaningful events in their life.

This kind of meeting is best done only with all the siblings present, not just some of them. It is a major mistake not to invite those who are more difficult for you to be with. They may have the most to offer you in the long run. Be cautious about trying this if there were some especially bitter or painful experiences in your family. In that case, some personal therapy might be called for first; then your therapist can help you plan the best approach to enlisting your siblings as a resource in the exploration of your family experiences.

The following worksheet of questions will help you think about your experience as a sibling. There are probably several hundred other questions like these that you could profitably ask yourself. Just remember to keep the focus on yourself and your part in any interactions. Look at how you might change, not how others should change.

To only children: Sorry that these questions about sibling relationships don't apply to you. You might instead use the questions to interview your parents and aunts and uncles about their childhood sibling experiences. You may learn something more about your childhood in the process.

WORKSHEET
EXPLORING YOUR EXPERIENCE AS A SIBLING

1. (a) What ways did you find to feel special in your family?

   (b) How did your family members (parents, siblings, grandparents) help with this?

   (c) Do you think that today you rely upon the same ways of feeling special, or have you changed these?

2. Did you enjoy your siblings? In what particular ways?

3. Were there any ways at all that you could provide support for each other?

4. (a) Did you enjoy and find support from all your siblings equally?

   (b) Who was the easiest and who was the most problematic for you?

5. (a) Which of your siblings did you react to with the most distress?

   (b) What was it that you reacted to most strongly?

   (c) What in you made you susceptible to this?

   (d) Were your other siblings as upset by this behavior as you were?

   (e) Can this sibling still get to you with the same behavior?

   (f) What has changed in you?

6. (a) Is there anyone in your life today who can get you stirred up in the same way as your most difficult sibling?

   (b) Do you find yourself behaving the same way with that person as you did with your sibling?

7. (a) What did you gain from your strife with a sibling at the time?

(b) Do you cash in on this with that sibling or with some-one else in that role now?

8. Did your relationship with your siblings, whether problematic or easy, help you develop some positive characteristics for living your life today? What are they?

9. (a) How did your parents handle your relationship with your siblings?

(b) How did they handle it when things got tense?

(c) How did you experience their intervention?

(d) When things get tense for you today in a problematic relationship, do you look for, or fear, the same kind of intervention from some other person?

(e) Did you get anything in particular from your parents when you and a sibling fought?

10. (a) Did you ever feel protective of, or protected by, one of your siblings?

(b) What particular behaviors did you engage in that elicited this protective behavior from your sibling?

(c) What behavior did your sibling engage in that stimu-lated you to be protective?

(d) Are these behaviors or dynamics at work in your cur-rent relationships?

11. (a) What did you learn about sharing or cooperation with your siblings?

(b) Did your parents help you learn these lessons? If so, how?

(c) To what extent do you take attitudes learned then into your current life situations and relationships?

12. (a) What was the best thing that your parents did that helped you with your relationship with your siblings?

(b)   What was the least helpful?

(c)   To what extent do you, as a parent (or as an em-
      ployer), repeat any of those actions?

13.   (a)   What kind of growth have you experienced in your
            sibling relationship over the years — especially as
            adults?

      (b)   What has helped that to happen?

      (c)   If there hasn't been growth, what do you think is
            keeping you stuck?

14.   (a)   Did your parents try to push you and your siblings to-
            gether and have you be buddies or best friends?

      (b)   What was the impact of this on you?

      (c)   How does it affect you today?

15.   (a)   Were differences among you and your siblings re-
            spected and even celebrated?

      (b)   Was it okay, or normal, to be different or were you
            pushed to be the same?

      (c)   What do you think was the impact of either of these
            two things?

16.   (a)   How important was your sibling relationship in
            terms of defining your own identity?

      (b)   How much of who you are today is based on the kind
            of relationship you had with each other?

      (c)   How do you think you would be different if you had
            a different sibling position?

      (d)   What do you think you could be doing now to over-
            come the things about yourself you don't like that are
            the result of your particular sibling experience?

17.   (a)   How were negative feelings handled in your family,
            and especially in your relationship with your sib-
            lings? For example, was anger allowed?

(b) How could it be expressed?

(c) What was not allowed?

(d) How well could your parents listen to your negative feelings?

(e) How well can you now listen to the negative feelings of others?

18. (a) Did your parents draw comparisons between you and your siblings?

(b) What was the result of this?

(c) How do you react today when you are compared to someone else?

(d) What kind of thoughts and feelings did you have about yourself and about your siblings when your parents made comparisons between you?

19. (a) Did your parents have favorites (most parents are more partial to one child than to others)?

(b) Did they show their favoritism (did they act on their feelings)? How?

20. Very often the favorite child is one of these: one who has the same sibling position as the parent; one who is in the same position as that of a parent's own favorite sibling; one who has a disability (the Tiny Tim syndrome). What seemed to be the basis of favoritism in your family?

21. (a) Do you know which sibling could stir up the most anxiety in your parents?

(b) What made each parent particularly sensitive to this sibling's behavior?

(c) How did the rest of you tend to respond when the parent got upset over this child's behavior?

(d) What was the impact of the response on you and the others?

22. (a) If your parents were able to recognize that each child had different needs and gave to each according to this standard (rather than giving the same to all, in order to be equal) how did this work for you and your siblings?

   (b) Did your difference from the others feel unique and special to you or did you think you had to be the same as your siblings to be liked and accepted?

23. (a) Did your parents tend to see you as having different abilities?

   (b) Was this helpful or not?

   (c) What made it one way or the other?

   (d) Did you try to cast yourself in a particular role with your parents? How did that go for you?

   (e) What was your role?

   (f) Do you know what went on in the family that made it seem you needed a role?

24. Did you play a role with your siblings that was unrelated to your parents and what they thought, felt, or wanted?

25. (a) Did you tend to go with your role or fight it? How did that work for you?

   (b) How are you doing with this role today in other relationships?

   (c) Are you still playing your family role or have you been able to broaden your way of being in the world to other styles and roles?

   (d) What would your partner say about 25(c)?

26. (a) Were you or one of your siblings a "problem child"?

   (b) What could be avoided or not dealt with as a result of being "a problem"?

27. (a) What were the ways your parents helped you resolve fights and conflicts?

    (b) What did you learn from this?

28. (a) Were you or one of your siblings a confidant to a parent?

    (b) How did this work?

    (c) What was the impact of this relationship on each of you?

29. Did one parent talk to you about one of your siblings and say things to you about him or her that were not said directly to the sibling? What was the impact of this on you, on your sibling, and on your relationship with that sibling?

30. (a) To what extent are you still carrying around hurt feelings from past interactions with your siblings?

    (b) How does it help you to have those feelings today (what do you not have to do or be)?

    (c) What would happen if you didn't have them?

    (d) How could you make them more intense and upsetting?

31. (a) What happened in the rest of the family whenever you and a sibling became closer or more distant emotionally?

    (b) Who seemed to get uneasy about this movement (in either direction) and how did he or she handle it?

32. (a) Are you cut off now from a sibling?

    (b) How did that come about?

    (c) What is the ongoing impact of this lack of contact?

    (d) What would have to change for you to reach out to him or her?

APPENDIX
BASIS OF RESEARCH

The descriptions of the various birth and sex orders summarized in this book are based on the research and writings of many authorities in the field, who between them have done hundreds of studies on the effects of birth order on personality development. Among them is Walter Toman, an Austrian psychologist, who has probably done the most extensive and comprehensive research in this area. He studied thousands of "normal" families and consistently found that people who were in the same birth and gender position had similar characteristics. He has been able to accurately guess a person's birth and gender order on the basis of a brief description of the person's personality. The results of his research are reported in his book, *Family Constellation: Its Effect on Personality and Social Behavior* (Springer, 1992).

Many other researchers and psychologists have come to similar conclusions about birth order characteristics. "The position in the family leaves an indelible stamp," said Alfred Adler, whose work preceded Toman's by several decades. Although some researchers, such as Lucille K. Forer, have used a different approach in studying birth order, there are more common findings than not, and they support the authors' own observations, particularly in Ron's clinical experience with families in therapy.

There is also some disagreement in the field about the validity of standard birth order descriptions. Judith Blake, for instance, has done extensive research and study on achievement and educational levels (see *Family Size and Achievement,* University of California Press, 1989), and she questions much of the previous research on birth order.

She says that the results that have been interpreted as having to do with birth order could be attributed to other factors not taken into account in the research. For instance, the fact that so many oldest children were among first-year university students in a particular year could merely reflect the high number of births 18 years previously and the number of smaller families in the population, which creates a proportionately larger number of oldest children.

For another example of questionable research conclusions, she points to a Dutch study that found much lower intelligence test scores among youngest children. What the study did not take into account, she says, were the economic and historical conditions that could have affected the outcome. Most of the youngest children in that study were born during severe wartime conditions in Holland when famine was widespread. The physical effects of malnourishment and the emotional effects of war rather than birth order could have caused the test results. However, without knowing how many of the youngest children were directly affected by those war-time conditions, it's impossible to know the effects of that variable.

Blake concludes on the basis of her work that there is no difference in cognitive abilities among the birth orders and that educational levels have more to do with the size of the family than birth order, with higher levels attained in small families, where for instance, all the children are likely to graduate from high school or university, or whatever the standard is for that family. In larger families, she found, the oldest and the youngest are likely to advance the farthest, with the middle children receiving less encouragement and fewer of the family resources.

Since Blake looked only at the level of education attained, not the standing of the students, it could still be true that the oldest children excelled and went on to more successful careers while the youngest children barely graduated. For instance, another study of scholastic ability in England found that only children, male and female, were the highest achievers, followed by eldest boys, eldest girls, youngest girls, youngest boys, middle boys, and middle girls, which is reflective of the traits usually ascribed to these birth orders.

However, as Blake rightly points out, ambition and achievement have more to do with the educational level and class of the parents than family size or birth order. And Walter Toman, too, notes that intelligence levels are similar in the same family, but that grades and occupational success vary according to birth order. Do not confuse what is called "intelligence" with a person's level of achievement or "success" in life; they are not equivalents.

Frank J. Sulloway systematically studied the lives of 6,000 North American and European scientists and found that their birth order was a highly significant factor in their acceptance or rejection of radical new theories. Allowing for many other variables, he consistently found that oldest (or functional oldests) were more conventional in their thinking and less willing to accept scientific innovations. And youngests were most likely to propose and accept startling new theories, regardless of the controversy created. His analysis of how birth order affects personality development is consistent with other findings in the field.

In large part, Toman's conclusions about the characteristics of men and women based on their sex and birth order reflect an old-fashioned and more European concept of masculine and feminine roles in the family (dominant men/passive women, for example). However, it is true that even today children are being brought up along similar lines. Certainly most people who are middle-aged and older adults today were brought up that way. Even the most liberated of us are affected by the subtle and not so subtle influences of society's old expectations about what

men and women are like. Even those who have outwardly overcome early sex-role stereotyping are, at their deepest emotional
level, sometimes still controlled by it.

If future generations succeed in bringing up children to be
whole human beings with the best of both masculine and feminine traits in both sexes, these standard, historical descriptions
of birth order traits will undoubtedly change. Relationships between the sexes will be different as well, and then sex and birth
order may have less drastic effects on how well we function.

BIBLIOGRAPHY

a. PSYCHOLOGY

Adler, Alfred. *Understanding Human Nature*. New York: Greenberg, 1946.

Alexander, Terry Pink. *Make Room for Twins*. Toronto: Bantam, 1987.

Arnstein, Helene S. *Brothers and Sisters/Sisters and Brothers*. New York: E. P. Dutton, 1979.

Bank, Stephen P., and Michael D. Kahn. *The Sibling Bond*. New York: Basic Books, 1982.

Blake, Judith. *Family Size and Achievement*. Berkeley: University of California Press, 1992.

Cassill, Kay. *Twins: Nature's Amazing Mystery*. New York: Atheneum, 1982.

Chess, Stella, and Alexander Thomas. *Temperament in Clinical Practice*. New York: The Guilford Press, 1986.

Dreikurs, Rudolf, and Loren Grey. *A Parents' Guide to Child Discipline*. New York: Hawthorn Books, 1970.

Easterlin, Richard A. *Birth and Fortune*. New York: Basic Books, 1980.

Faber, Adele, and Elaine Mazlish. *Siblings Without Rivalry: How to Help Your Children Live Together so You Can Live Too*. New York: W. W. Norton, 1987.

Forer, Lucille K., and Henry Still. *The Birth Order Factor: How Your Personality Is Influenced by Your Place in the Family.* New York: David McKay, 1976.

Forer, Lucille K. *Birth Order and Life Roles*. Springfield, Illinois: Charles C. Thomas, 1969.

Freud, Sigmund. *Introductory Lectures on Psychoanalysis*. New York: Norton, 1929, 1965.

Friedrich, Elizabeth, and Cherry Rowland. *The Parents' Guide to Raising Twins*. New York: St. Martin's Press, 1983.

Hoopes, Margaret M., and James M. Harper. *Birth Order Roles and Sibling Patterns in Individual and Family Therapy.* Rockville, Maryland: Aspen Publishers, 1987.

Isaacson, Clifford E. *The Birth Order Challenge: Expanding Your Horizons*. Algoma, Iowa: Upper Des Moines Counseling Center, 1991.

Kappelman, Murray. *Raising the Only Child*. New York: E.P. Dutton, 1975.

Konig, Karl. *Brothers and Sisters: The Order of Birth in the Family.* New York: Anthroposophic Press, 1963.

Leman, Kevin. *The New Birth Order Book*. Old Tappan, New Jersey: Fleming H. Revell, 1999.

McGoldrick, Monica. *You Can Go Home Again: Reconnecting with Your Family.* New York: W.W. Norton & Co., 1997.

McGoldrick, Monica, Carol M. Anderson, and Froma Walsh, eds. *Women in Families: A Framework for Family Therapy.* New York: W.W. Norton, 1989.

Nachman, Patricia. *You and Your Only Child: The Joys, Myths and Challenges of Raising an Only Child.* New York: HarperCollins, 1997.

Neisser, Edith G. *Brothers and Sisters.* New York: Harper and Brothers, 1951.

Novotny, Pamela Patrick. *The Joy of Twins: Having, Raising, and Loving Babies Who Arrive in Groups.* New York: Crown, 1988.

Pogrebin, Letty Cottin. *Growing Up Free: Raising Your Child in the 80's.* New York: McGraw-Hill, 1980.

Sifford, Darrell. *The Only Child: Being One, Loving One, Understanding One, Raising One.* New York: G.P. Putnam's Sons, 1990.

Somit, Albert, Steven A. Peterson, and Alan Arwine. *Birth Order and Political Behavior.* University Press of America, 1995.

Sulloway, Frank J. *Born to Rebel: Birth Order, Family Dynamics and Creative Lives.* New York: Random House, 1997.

Sutton-Smith, Brian, and B.G. Rosenberg. *The Sibling.* New York: Holt, Rinehart and Winston, 1970.

Toman, Walter. *Family Constellation: Its Effects on Personality and Social Behavior.* 4th ed. New York: Jason Aronson, 1995.

Wallace, Meri. *Birth Order Blues: How Parents Can Help Their Children Meet the Challenges of Their Birth Order.* New York: Henry Holt & Co., 1999.

Wilson, Bradford, and George Edington. *First Child, Second Child: Your Birth Order Profile.* New York: McGraw-Hill, 1981.

Wilson, Colin. *New Pathways in Psychology: Maslow and the Post-Freudian Revolution.* New York: Taplinger, 1972.

b. AUTOBIOGRAPHIES AND BIOGRAPHIES

Adamson, Joy. *The Searching Spirit.* New York: Harcourt Brace Jovanovich, 1978.

Andersen, Hans Christian. *The Fairy Tale of My Life.* New York: Paddington Press Ltd., 1975.

Asimov, Isaac. *In Memory Yet Green*. New York: Doubleday, 1979.

Banks, Kerry. *Pavel Bure: The Riddle of the Russian Rocket*. Vancouver: Douglas & McIntyre, 1999.

Bergman, Ingrid. *Ingrid Bergman: My Story.* New York: Delacorte Press, 1980.

Berton, Pierre. *Starting Out, 1920-1947*. Toronto: McClelland & Stewart, 1987.

Canning, John. *100 Great Modern Lives*. London: Odhams Books, 1967.

Caro, Robert A. *The Years of Lyndon Johnson: The Path to Power.* New York: Alfred A. Knopf, 1982.

Carpenter, Humphrey. *W. H. Auden: A Biography.* Boston: Houghton Mifflin, 1981.

Cathcart, Helen. *Prince Charles*. London: W. H. Allen, 1976.

Cate, Curtis. *Antoine de Saint-Exupery: His Life and Times.* New York: G.P. Putnam's Sons, 1970.

Chalfont, Alun. *Montgomery of Alamein*. New York: Atheneum, 1976.

Church, Richard. *Over the Bridge*. London: The Reprint Society, 1955.

Clark, Ronald W. *Einstein: The Life and Times*. New York: Avon Books, 1984.

Cohen-Solal, Annie. *Sartre: A Life*. New York: Pantheon, 1987.

Current Biography Yearbook. New York: H.W. Wilson, various years.

Davies, Hunter. *The Beatles*. London: Heinemann, 1968.

de Beauvoir, Simone. *Memoirs of a Dutiful Daughter.* New York: Harper & Row, 1958.

Dillard, Annie. *An American Childhood*. New York: Harper & Row, 1987.

Donahue, Phil. *My Own Story.* New York: Simon and Schuster, 1979.

Duberman, Martin Bauml. *Paul Robeson.* New York: Alfred A. Knopf, 1988.

Du Maurier, Daphne. *The Du Mauriers.* New York: Literary Guild of America, 1937.

Durant, Will, and Ariel Durant. *Will and Ariel Durant: A Dual Autobiography.* New York: Simon and Schuster, 1977.

Fonteyn, Margot. *Margot Fonteyn: Autobiography.* London: W. H. Allan, 1975.

Frank, Anne. *The Diary of a Young Girl.* New York: Simon and Schuster, 1987.

Friedrich, Otto. *Glenn Gould: A Life and Variations.* New York: Simon & Schuster, 1990.

Goodwin, Doris Kearns. *The Fitzgeralds and the Kennedys: An American Saga.* New York: Simon and Schuster, 1987.

Higham, Charles. *Kate: The Life of Katharine Hepburn.* New York: W.W. Norton, 1975.

Higham, Charles. *Lucy: The Real Life of Lucille Ball.* New York: St. Martin's, 1986.

Holden, Anthony. *Prince Charles.* New York: Atheneum, 1979.

Hove, Ralphe E. *Dorothy L. Sayers: A Literary Biography.* Kent State, Ohio: The Kent State University Press, 1979.

Huxley, Elspeth. *Florence Nightingale.* New York: G. P. Putnam, 1975.

Keller, Helen. *Story of My Life.* Garden City: Doubleday, 1905.

Kirkup, James. *The Only Child: An Autobiography of Infancy.* London: Collins, 1957.

Lacey, Robert. *Majesty.* New York: Harcourt Brace, 1977.

Lee, Laurie. *Cider with Rosie.* London: Hogarth Press, 1978.

Lee, Laurie. *I Can't Stay Long*. London: Andre Deutsch, 1975.

Lenburg, Jeff. *Dustin Hoffman: Hollywood's Antihero*. New York: St. Martin's, 1983.

Lenzner, Robert. *The Great Getty: The Life and Loves of J. Paul Getty, the Richest Man in the World*. New York: Crown, 1976.

Lyons, Eugene. *David Sarnoff: A Biography*. New York: Harper & Row, 1966.

Martin, Ralph G. *Golda: The Romantic Years*. New York: Charles Scribner's Sons, 1988.

Mazlish, Bruce, and Edwin Diamond. *Jimmy Carter: An Interpretive Biography*. New York: Simon and Schuster, 1979.

Mead, Margaret. *Blackberry Winter: My Earlier Years*. New York William Morrow & Company, 1972.

Meir, Golda. *My Life*. London: Weidenfeld & Nicholson, 1975.

Miller, Arthur. *Timebends*. New York: Grove Press, 1987.

Morley, Sheridan. *The Other Side of the Moon*. London: Weidenfeld and Nicolson, 1985.

Mortimer, John. *Clinging to the Wreckage: A Part of Life*. New York: Penguin, 1984.

Oates, Stephen B. *Let the Trumpet Sound: The Life of Martin Luther King, Jr.* New York: Harper and Row, 1982.

Paine, Albert Bigelow. *The Boy's Life of Mark Twain*. New York: Harper and Row, 1944.

Pauck, Wilhelm and Marion. *Paul Tillich: His Life and Thought*. Vol. 1: Life. New York: Harper and Row, 1976.

Pavarotti, Luciano, with William Wright. *Pavarotti: My Own Story*. Garden City, NY: Doubleday, 1981.

Pollock, John. *Billy Graham*. London: Hodder and Stoughton, 1966.

Price, Reynolds. *Clear Pictures: First Love, First Guides.* New York: Atheneum, 1989.

Reagan, Ronald. *An American Life: The Autobiography.* New York: Simon & Schuster, 1990.

Robbins, Jhan. *Bess and Harry: An American Love Story.* New York: G.P. Putnam's Sons, 1980.

Shaw, George Bernard. *Shaw: An Autobiography 1856-1898.* New York: Waybright and Talley, 1969.

Sheehy, Gail. *Hillary's Choice.* New York: Random House, 1999.

Sills, Beverly, and Lawrence Linderman. *Beverly: An Autobiography.* New York: Bantam, 1987.

Spalding, Frances. *Stevie Smith: A Critical Biography.* London: Faber & Faber, 1988.

Stirling, Monica. *The Wild Swan.* London: Collins, 1965.

Taylor, John Russell. *Hitch: The Life and Times of Alfred Hitchcock.* New York: Pantheon Books, 1978.

Updike, John. *Self-Consciousness.* New York: Alfred A. Knopf, 1989.

Ustinov, Peter. *Dear Me.* Boston, Toronto: Little, Brown, 1977.

Waterfield, Lina. *Castle in Italy: An Autobiography.* London: John Murray, 1961.

boy/younger girl relationship approximates the stereotypical husband/wife combination.

The oldest brother of sisters believes life and love are important, and he is, in some ways, a hedonist, but usually a considerate, unselfish one. He usually wants a peaceful life and tends to be realistic about what is possible, without taking too many risks. He may be gallant as well as good-natured. If his sister was considered the emotional one, he is likely to be more dignified and reserved. He is a good steward of his possessions, but isn't usually concerned about accumulating great wealth. He would rather spend time with his family than work hard to make more money or be more successful.

If there are four or five years between them, the oldest brother of sisters is not threatened by the birth of a mere girl, so usually grows up less hostile and less competitive than an oldest brother of brothers.

Since in most families he is still the favored child by virtue of gender, he has less need to compete with his younger sibling. He may start acting more masculine and belittle the girl's weakness just to be sure he retains his advantage, but usually this isn't necessary. Violinist Yehudi Menuhin, with two talented younger sisters who were piano prodigies, was easily able to maintain his pre-eminent position in the family.

If they are quite close in age, the oldest brother of a sister may not realize there is a difference in sex or understand the implications of the difference. In that case, he will feel jealousy at least until he becomes aware of his good fortune in being a male. He may repress his jealousy, picking up at some level that it's not the appropriate emotion for an oldest brother of a sister to feel. If he keeps that feeling and other feelings buried for too long, he may always have difficulty revealing his secret thoughts and fears. He often develops physical ailments to get mother's attention without appearing to fight for it.

Although he is usually more attached to his mother, he needs to have a father he can look up to and admire. If his own father doesn't fill this role, he will look for other men who will.

Depending on the kind of relationship his parents have, he may be very protective toward his sister and be her confidante and a willing teacher about life.

> A year after the family's arrival in Munich, Albert's sister Maja was born. Only two years younger, she was to become constant companion and unfailing confidante....he faced the loss of two wives with equanimity; but the death of his sister, at the age of 70, dented the hard defensive shell he had built around his personal feelings.

> Ronald W. Clark, *Einstein: The Life and Times*

If his sister seems like a pest as a child, he may just ignore her or he may be remarkably tolerant of her, which makes him too willing to accept the petulant behavior of adult women he may be attracted to later in life.

Barry was the oldest brother of two sisters. He married an only child who was used to being the princess in her family. Whatever she didn't want to do, as a wife, mother, housekeeper (which was quite a lot), fell to Barry who picked it up without a complaint. Without any sense of what was going on with him, Barry became significantly depressed and much less functional. His wife was upset by it, and he thought he was a failure. He resisted his therapist's urgings to have his wife share in the therapy. Barry insisted it was just his problem.

During the course of therapy, Barry began to be aware of his own needs and what he wanted from his wife. His depression began to lift as he started expressing these needs. His wife could see the legitimacy of his requests, but was not emotionally prepared herself to meet them. They mutually decided to end their marriage, with Barry having custody of their eight-year-old daughter. Barry was warned about the danger of getting into the same kind of pattern with her.

The oldest brother of sisters may have had the experience of being waited on by his younger sister (and mother), and in that case will expect other women to cater to him. But in almost all cases he is kind and considerate to women.

He may have expected his sister to be like him and have been impatient that she was relatively so weak, but generally he is very fond of all women. Luciano Pavarotti, oldest brother of a sister and adored by his close-knit extended family, is a shining example of this. According to *Luciano Pavarotti: My Own Story,* Pavarotti's sister says of him that he has "a special thing for women...beyond the normal, warm-blooded Italian male response." He renovated an old house in Italy so he could have his whole family living there, including his wife's sister and her family and his sister and her child, before he left his first wife for a younger woman.

2.   As a spouse

The oldest brother of sisters can have a good marriage with a woman from almost any birth order, though the most comfortable is usually with the youngest sister of brothers, which duplicates exactly the situation he is used to. If he was too domineering with his sister or his wife was rebellious toward her older brother, they run the risk of repeating those patterns.

When he marries the oldest sister of brothers, there are often conflicts over who is the leader, but the arrival of children usually lessens their competition — unless they start competing over being the best parent.

The youngest sister of sisters may submit to his authority, but she is often too prissy for his tastes.

An only child is sometimes an acceptable match, since she is still the baby in her family and can appreciate his taking care of her. The oldest sister of sisters is the most difficult match, though he can often handle it anyway since he is accustomed to pleasing all females.

He is often a romantic and puts his wife and family first in his priorities. However, the more sisters he has and the closer he was to his mother, the more difficult it is for him to settle for just one woman as a partner.

...young Paul adored his mother. "My whole life was embedded in her," he once said. "I couldn't imagine any other woman." Shortly before her death [at age 45] he said to her, "I would like to marry you."

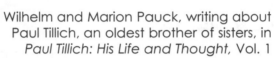

He continued to worship her...and sought her forever after in every [woman] he pursued....Tillich and his sister Johanna drew exceedingly close to each other...she became his ideal.

Wilhelm and Marion Pauck, writing about Paul Tillich, an oldest brother of sisters, in *Paul Tillich: His Life and Thought,* Vol. 1

3.   As a parent

In any match, the wife of an oldest brother of sisters is usually more important to him than his children. However, he usually wants children, to complete the family, and is often a good father — loving and concerned about his children, but not overly strict.

If there are children of both sexes who are in the same birth positions as the parents, especially an older boy and younger girl, they usually all get along together happily.

4.   As a friend

The oldest brother of sisters is not usually "one of the boys" with male friends, though he is on good terms with most men. He is least likely to be friends with another oldest brother of sisters: both are more interested in the other's sisters. The more sisters he has, the fewer male friends he usually has.